NAURU ISLAND

TIMOR SEA

CORAL SEA

PACIFIC OCEAN

NORFOLK ISLAND

LORD HOWE ISLAND

TASMAN SEA

BASS STRAIT

SOUTHERN OCEAN

MACQUARIE ISLAND

ANTARCTICA

ISLANDS OF AUSTRALIA

SLANDS OF AUSTRALIA

DOUGLASS BAGLIN and
BARBARA MULLINS

Designed by
BERYL GREEN

URE SMITH·SYDNEY

Cover photographs:
Front, Ball's Pyramid, fantastic peak of sheer
rock which rises vertically from the ocean
depths near Lord Howe Island. Remnant of an
ancient volcano, most dramatic of all the
Pacific islands, it soars to a height of
1850 feet above sea-level from a base of
only three-quarters of an acre. **Back,** Buccaneer
Archipelago, in Yampi Sound, bay of a thousand
islands. Named for British buccaneer William
Dampier who landed here in 1688, these are indeed
the golden islands of the west; they are islands
of pure iron, a major source of Western Australia's
booming mineral wealth.

First published in Australia 1970
by Horwitz Publications
This edition published in Australia 1972
by Ure Smith Pty Limited
176 South Creek Road, Dee Why West 2099
Reprinted November 1972
Copyright © Douglass Baglin (photography)
Barbara Mullins (text), 1970, 1972
National Library of Australia Card
Number and ISBN 0 7254 0084 6
Designed and typeset in Australia
Printed in Hong Kong by
Toppan Printing Company (H.K.) Limited
All rights reserved

Foreword

Islands have a special fascination for most people. Perhaps they appeal to Robinson Crusoe qualities that linger on long after childhood has gone. Maybe it is because there is often adventure or unpredictableness involved in getting to our island, so we feel intrepid on arrival. Then it is so easy to cast aside cares and worries on an island–especially one free of those twin menaces of modern civilization, the telephone and news media.

This very cut-offness seems to set them apart, so that islanders develop great qualities of self sufficiency and self reliance and they tend to become a little bit different from their neighbours on the mainland or even from those on other nearby islands. How different are the people of the Bass Strait Islands and those from the islands of Arnhem Land in the north! Even Lord Howe and Norfolk Islanders who, Pacific-wise, are near neighbours, differ in many subtle ways in their lives and outlooks. What causes these differences in people? Is it the geology and geographical situation or the weather and climate that moulds them, or is it some other special "island" factor?

To naturalists, islands are of particular interest and, in a way, bear the same sort of relationship to large nearby land masses as do rock pools to the sea. Each is a small, somewhat restricted sample of the larger body from which its biota derives, and it is intriguing to try and work out the why and wherefore of these restrictions and how the flora and fauna came to be the way they are. We find that each island is different according to its geology, history, area and distance from its main source of colonisation. These are the factors reflected in this book, and the photographs convey, so much more than thousands of words could, the kinds of places our islands are.

Barbara Mullins and Douglass Baglin take us on a voyage among the thousands of islands around Australia and its dependencies. Within the framework of a broad geographic picture they have selected a series of islands and groups to show a variety of end results of island "evolutions." In so large an area it would be impossible to depict all the islands, or to investigate all the aspects of even one of those chosen, but by treating the islands as groups, and emphasising some outstanding features that they share–for example, muttonbirds and those that seek them, in the islands of Bass Strait, treasure troves of history, fauna and mineral wealth in the islands of the west–the authors manage very well to show the types of islands around Australia, and the island peoples that live on them.

To anyone like myself, who suffers from a sort of mild "island fever," this book is most welcome and I can commend it to anyone interested in history, natural history or earth sciences–or just plain islands.

Elizabeth C. Pope,
M.Sc., F.R.Z.S., C.M.Z.S.
Curator of Worms and Echinoderms,
The Australian Museum.

Previous pages: *Strangler fig clambers up towering rainforest tree on Fraser Island, massive sand dune isolated by rising seas of the last ice age.*

Moon over Hinchinbrook, largest of the high islands which skirt the coastline of northern Queensland. They are the peaks of drowned mountains, relics of a by-gone coastal range.

Children of Bathurst Island, Arnhem Land, play in a dugout canoe made from hollowed tree.

This page: *Sooty petrel rising at dawn from a rock platform on Cat Island, Bass Strait — the start of a long trans-equatorial flight northward across the Pacific to the Bering Sea.*

Contents

Furneaux Group · Cat Island · Babel Island · Cape Barren Island
Storehouse Island · Preservation Island · Moriarty Rocks
Clark Island · Fisher Island · Flinders Island · King Island

ISLANDS OF BASS STRAIT

Tobias Furneaux, who, in command of *Adventure,* accompanied James Cook on his second voyage, was the first European known to view Bass Strait, and he mistook it for a wide and treacherous bay – "nothing but islands and shoals; the land high, rocky and barren," he wrote in March, 1773, and named the area "Bay of Shoals." He was in fact sailing across the eastern end of the strait, among the islands which now commemorate his name – the Furneaux Group. Then in 1797 the *Sydney Cove* was wrecked on Preservation Island, an event which precipitated exploration of Bass Strait, led directly to the great sealing rush of the first decade of last century, and profoundly changed the course of history on the islands of Bass Strait.

The islands of Bass Strait are remnants of two land bridges which once linked Tasmania to the mainland. One embraced King Island at the western end of the strait – it is believed that the Yarra in Victoria and the Tamar in Tasmania then joined in a mighty river which flowed into the Southern Ocean between King Island and Cape Otway on the mainland. The eastern link extended from Wilson's Promontory across the bay of shoals to the Furneaux Group and northeastern Tasmania. These land bridges appeared and disappeared at intervals over a million years or more, permitting migration of flora and fauna between Tasmania and the mainland, allowing specialisation to develop in the period that the islands were isolated. As would be expected, the flora on the islands includes species common to both sides of Bass Strait – *Eucalyptus globulus,* the southern blue gum, floral emblem of Tasmania, occurs also on the mainland in some south coast areas and is (or was, before the forests were cleared) common on the islands of Bass Strait. *Epacris impressa,* the floral emblem of Victoria, is another example; this also occurs on the islands and was first described from Tasmania. Other island species are fully endemic, easily distinguishable from their nearest mainland relatives.

The fauna also shows links with the mainland, marked by speciation and survival of species only possible in the isolation of islands and tragically vulnerable to invasion. Islands are natural laboratories, sanctuaries and museums, but the very factors that enable unique fauna to develop or survive long after their mainland counterparts have become extinct, convert them, once invaded, into natural slaughter-pens from which there is no escape. Fur seals were slaughtered last century like "hogs in a pound," to quote a contemporary source, and the huge sea-elephants which once abounded in the area were soon exterminated – the species survives now only in the sanctuary of sub-Antarctic islands hundreds of miles to the south. The dwarr black emu of King Island did not long survive the arrival of early sealers and the subsequent destruction of the mighty eucalypt forests. But seabirds are the symbol of the isles of Bass Strait, and these still breed there in numbers, drawn by that strange, life-long attachment which most ocean-rovers have for the isolated islands or even wave-washed rocks where their life began.

Face of a fisherman reflects the rugged conditions and stormy history of the islands of Bass Strait.

Rock formations, Storehouse Island, stained orange and rusty red by encrustations of lichen, Gasparinnia murolum. This is the characteristic colour of the islands.

Soft balls of dusky down — mutton bird chicks on Cat Island. These are the harvest of the moon-birders, taken by hand from burrows, threaded onto spits by the beak so that oil stored in their crops does not ooze out.

The birds of the moon take off before daybreak on an April morn. Truly oceanic, they range the wide Pacific from Bass Strait to the Bering Sea.

Tussock grass shields the burrows of nesting mutton birds. Cray boats ride at anchor in the bay. (Cat Island)

Scientists call them *Puffinus tenuirostris,* but they are birds of many names . . .
Captain Cook called them "black sheer-waters," and with a gannet, an "Egg Bird" (sooty tern) and "several Albetrosses," they heralded the nearness of land and the discovery of the east coast of Australia. Matthew Flinders, eighteen years later, called them petrels, and marvelled at the millions which darkened the sky: "There was a stream of from fifty to eighty yards in depth," he wrote, "and of three hundred yards, or more, in breadth. The birds were not scattered but flying as compactly as a free movement of their wings seemed to allow, and during a full hour and a half this stream of petrels continued to pass without interruption . . . On the lowest computation I think the number could not have been less than a hundred million."
Poets call them petrels, too; the name is derived from St. Peter, an allusion to an illusion, for these birds appear to walk on water. They skim low over the waves, feet cleaving the sea's surface, and owe the name "shearwater" also to this habit.
Those that sought them for their succulent flesh called them mutton birds, or even "flying sheep." The late Professor F. Wood Jones, eminent zoologist and author who spent many years in Australia, named them the birds of the moon. Alluding to the age-old theory that the moon was made from the substance of the earth, and would well fit into the Pacific void, he wrote: "And when the Moon went from the Earth what happened? Did she carry to a cold death a whole realm of earth's life? Did she leave homeless some creatures that had made their home upon her terrestrial surface? In the whole array of living things there is only one terrestrial order that is homeless and is alien in any land—only one group that lives upon no continental mass, but owns the Moon-void as its playground, and its scattered islands as its only home. Every island of the Moon-void has its Petrel, and no Petrel comes to live on any continent. Truly the birds of St. Peter are birds of the moon. Of all birds they are children of the Pacific void and have moon-time for all their activities . . ."

Adult Australian gannet with chicks.
In former years Cat Island supported the
largest known rookeries of these birds,
but raids by cray fishers seeking nestlings
for bait have almost exterminated the
breeding population; in March, 1969 the
author saw only six pairs.

Forests of giant kelp, Sarcophycus
potatorum, fringe the rocky coast of Cat
Island; fragments are cast upon the sandy
shores as sea wrack, there to be gathered
by gannets and wrought into neat,
cone-shaped nests.

Mutton bird shelters in tussock grass, ·
Cat Island. These seafarers of the Pacific
are known by many names: Tasmanian
mutton bird, short-tailed shearwater,
sooty petrel and bird of the moon; each
name carries a story.

Steve Walker banding mutton birds on
Cat Island. Much has been learnt about
bird migration and behaviour
by this means.

Venomous black tiger snakes, Notechis
scutatus niger, abound on the bird islands,
often taking up residence in burrows
of mutton birds.

Rock-strewn beach, Cat Island.

Flat-topped peak of Babel Island.

African box-thorn, Lycium ferocissimum, naturalised on Cat Island.

Channel between Cat and Babel Islands, Bass Strait. Fishermen shelter in lee of islands in bad weather.

The birds of the moon are indeed oceanic, only visiting their islands to nest and rear their young. Each spring they travel in great flocks to ancestral rookeries on the bird islands of Bass Strait; each winter they depart on their 10,000-mile journey to the fringe of the Arctic Circle, half a world away, tracing great figures of eight across the broad bosom of the Pacific. Their migration is triggered by sensitivity to day-length; in the seasonal progression from long summer days to the short day-length of winter, there is a "threshold level" which stimulates migration, and the great flocks take to the air, curving southwest to the islands of Bass Strait in September, and northeast to the Bering Sea in June. Australian poet Henry Kendall spoke of "September, the maid with the wind in her hair"; Bass Strait fishermen call those same September winds "mutton bird gales." They can predict, almost to the day or even the hour, the return of the birds of the moon to their traditional breeding grounds. Tasmanian mutton birds no longer occur in the astronomical numbers that Flinders recorded. Mass slaughter last century has taken a heavy toll. Even today, with eggs and mature birds strictly protected and the season for chicks restricted to six short weeks, the annual harvest in a good year can be up to half a million. But still the mutton bird gales of mid-September darken the skies with these dusky-brown birds, scarcely bigger than a pigeon, silently homing to their islands, often even to a particular burrow. There follows a frantic few weeks of spring-cleaning, raking out burrows anything up to four feet deep, evicting the venomous black tiger snakes that abound in the islands, repairing damage done by trampling cattle. Then off to sea again to recuperate before returning purposefully to their individual burrows to lay the solitary, large white egg. This the parents tend in shifts, each partner in turn brooding, foodless, for about a fortnight while the other builds up strength at sea. When the chick hatches it is fussed over by both, fed with regurgitated, partly digested food so lavishly that within a month it exceeds them in size. Soon after, with the approach of southern winter, the adult birds heed the age-old call to return to the Pacific void and summer in the north, leaving the chicks with crops full of fat, to live on their reserves until, hungry and restless, they shuffle along time-worn tracks to the nearest rocky headland and themselves take to the sea and northern summers. That is, if they do not fall harvest to the moon-birders.

The Australian gannet (Sula serrulata) ranges the southern seas of Australasia from Fremantle to New Zealand, but is known to breed only on a few small islands in Bass Strait, off southern Tasmania, and on the North Island of New Zealand. Until recent years the largest Australian gannet rookery was on Cat Island, where the birds congregated in great crowded colonies of two thousand or more breeding pairs. Today the precise rows of cone-shaped nests, lined with sea-wrack, grass and cast-off snake skins, are deserted and in ruins, for raids by cray fishers seeking bait have reduced the breeding population to only a few pairs.

Preservation Island, Furneaux Group. The Sydney Cove *was wrecked here in 1797. Survivors from it were the first white men to travel the coastal strip of south-eastern Australia.*

Treacherous shoals of the Furneaux Group are scattered with wrecks.

Australian fur seals, Arctocephalus doriferus, *on Moriarty Rocks, Furneaux Group. Bass Strait islands were major sealing grounds last century, and the animals were hunted almost to extinction. They are now protected.*

The tale of islands is a tale of shipwreck, and one of the most treacherous stretches of water in Bass Strait is Furneaux's "Bay of Shoals" which surrounds the island group Cook later named for him. "I think it is a very dangerous shore to fall in with," Furneaux wrote in 1773, and promptly turned eastward for New Zealand and his rendezvous with Cook. Indeed, Furneaux was convinced that there was no strait between Tasmania and the mainland, but only a wide and treacherous shoal-marred bay.

Perhaps the most incredible story of shipwreck in the Furneaux Group is that of the *Sydney Cove,* which left Bengal, under command of Captain Guy Hamilton, in November, 1796, with speculative cargo, bound for her namesake settlement on Port Jackson. She encountered strong gales and high seas, and by mid-January a serious leak had developed, which was treated by fothering–the method used earlier by Captain Cook to save *Endeavour* when she ran aground on the Barrier Reef. During another violent gale the second mate was lost from the yardarm. The ship laboured badly, the leak increased, the cold was intense. Three men dropped dead at the pump; it was impossible to keep the water under. There was four feet in the well, and the arduous task of bailing was regarded as a respite from other duties in the bitter blast. In this condition they rounded Van Diemen's Land, passed Maria Island, only to encounter more terrific gales and high seas. A fresh leak developed and gained so rapidly that much of the cargo was jettisoned. The ship was settling fast and, realizing she was doomed, the captain decided to beach her. Land was visible, two miles distant, fringed with forbidding rocks; the ship would scarcely answer the helm, owing to her water-logged condition. The captain nevertheless manoeuvred her ashore, and hardly had the crew reached safety in the longboat than the vessel sank in three fathoms. This was on that rocky island in the Furneaux Group later named Preservation. There was no

water, so they dug a well and managed with the brackish water they reached. Such stores and goods as it was possible to retrieve were got ashore. The longboat was equipped, and some of the crew embarked in an attempt to reach Sydney for assistance–Hugh Thompson, mate, W. Clarke, supercargo, three European seamen and twelve Lascars—seventeen men in all. The remainder settled down to await rescue.

Meanwhile, those in the longboat battled their way across stormy Bass Strait; as they neared the mainland the boat was swamped by heavy seas and went to pieces in the violent surf near Point Hicks, that "southernmost point of land" so-named by Cook for the man who first sighted the east coast of Australia (now called Cape Everard). Without provisions, without arms, the seventeen started on the 500-mile walk up the coast to Sydney. Only three of them survived the hazardous journey, and these were the first outsiders to gain knowledge of that long strip of coast. With the assistance of Aborigines, who seemed more eager to see them on their way than to harass them, they lived off the land, forded wide rivers such as the Shoalhaven, wandered around broad bays.

W. Clarke, the supercargo, kept a graphic diary containing a description of the country and the rivers they were obliged to cross. The going was desperately hard. On April 16th he wrote: "Our poor, unfortunate companions, worn out by want and excessive fatigue, began to drop behind fast. We were under the painful necessity of leaving nine of our fellow sufferers behind, they being unable to proceed further, but we thought they would be able to come up with us in a day or two as we were often delayed for some time with the natives, when we found them kind to us, or we loitered about the rocks to pick up shells or collect herbs . . ." The Aborigines were often unpredictable. On April 26th: "At 9 a.m. we observed several natives on the top of a high bluff who came down to us . . . When we had made signs to them that we were hungry and much exhausted they brought us plenty of fish and treated us very kindly . . . We had not parted from them for more than 20 or 30 minutes when 100 more approached us, shouting in a most hideous manner at which we were all much alarmed. In a short time they began throwing their spears at us . . ." But when on the 30th the party came to the largest river they had yet met with, natives appeared and assisted them to cross. For 15 more days they struggled on, growing gradually weaker, until on March 15th they sighted a fishing boat–they were then about 15 miles south of Botany Bay–and attracted its attention by making a large fire, using, it is believed, coal which they had discovered in abundance on the cliffs along the shore. They had been two months on their journey; Clarke and two sailors, one a Lascar, were the three survivors. Hugh Thompson and the ship's carpenter had dropped out shortly before the boat was sighted; their skeletons were found on a later search. Governor Hunter dispatched the colonial schooner *Francis*, first vessel launched in Sydney,

Opposite page: Cape Barren Island at sunset; lichen-stained balancing rock; wind-pruned tree, Coprosma repens.

This Page: Grass-trees, Xanthorrhoea australis var. australis, frame mist-shrouded Mount Nuroe. Lower picture: Strange rock formations, Cape Barren Island.

20

and the sloop-rigged boat *Eliza,* to the rescue of those left on Preservation Island, who had existed through four winter months, their only shelter from continuous heavy rain and cold gales being tents made from sails which were constantly blown down, their rations a meagre teacup of rice a day. The two vessels picked up survivors and, loaded with part of the cargo from the wreck, sailed for Sydney Cove. After a stormy passage of fifteen days *Francis* arrived safely but *Eliza* was separated and never heard of again.

"I sent in the schooner Lieut. Flinders, a young man well qualified, in order to give him an opportunity of making what observations he could amongst these islands," Hunter wrote, "and from the discoveries that were made there by him and Mr. Hamilton, the master of the wrecked ship, I presume that the land called Van Diemen's Land and generally supposed to be the southern promontory of this country, is a group of islands separated from the southern coast by a strait."

But this was not the end of the ramifications of the wreck of the *Sydney Cove.* Some months later Flinders' colleague, George Bass, set out in a whaleboat with six seamen, to make a more extensive survey and investigate survivors' reports of the area. He sighted smoke on an

The features of the lost Tasmanians are mirrored in the faces of the Cape Barren Islanders, but with each successive generation the image is fading. After the Black War last century the tragic remnants of Tasmanian Aborigines were exiled here; descendants are proud of their ancestry.

An air of brooding hostility hangs over this old home on Cape Barren Island. Outsiders are not welcome. The architecture of the islands, like the people, reflects a mixture of racial influences.

Trees and misty hills of Cape Barren Island; tall blue gums, Eucalyptus globulus (above) contrast with wind-moulded low growth (below).

Dr. D. L. Serventy seeks mutton bird chicks for banding. Birds have been known to return to the burrows in which they were hatched.

Fisher Island, Furneaux Group, site of Yolla, C.S.I.R.O. Research Station.

Dom Serventy near landing ramp at Yolla, where he has spent many years.

Unusual weathered rock, Fisher Island, sculptured by wind and sea.

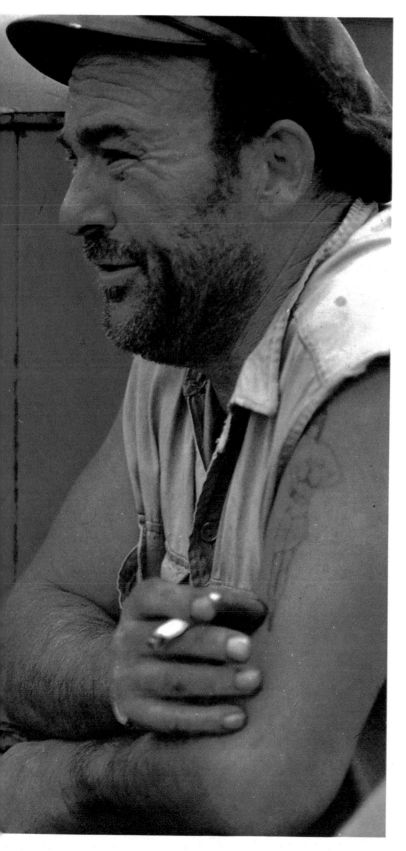

Old cattle-loading ramp on Clarke Island, Bass Strait; sailing ships loaded here — the cattle swam out and were hauled aboard.

Clarke Island farmer. Islanders of the Furneaux Group tend small herds of sheep and cattle, usually supplemented by seasonal cray fishing and mutton birding.

island near the point of land he named Wilson Promontory, and discovered a party of escaped convicts. Three months earlier they had stolen a boat from Sydney in an attempt to reach the *Sydney Cove,* which they hoped to refloat and sail for some destination safe from the law. Bass brought two of them back to Sydney in the whaleboat; the others were landed on the mainland with a musket and some supplies, so that they might, if possible, make their way along the coast to the colony, in the wake of the *Sydney Cove* survivors. They were never heard of again. Perhaps they managed to make a place for themselves among the natives, as did Buckley, the "wild white man," who joined the Aborigines of Port Phillip a few years later and lived with them for thirty-two years.

Shipwrecked mariners, escaped convicts–what else for the islands of Bass Strait, which once knew only the cry of the sea birds, the surge of wind and wave, the seasonal visits of the huge seal populations which then roamed our southern seas? In the wake of the navigators flocked sealers from the seven seas, carrying with them captive women of the South Pacific, combing every wave-washed rock and isle for its harvest of furs and oil. The early years of last century were marked by vast abundance, easy hunting and massive slaughter. Single ships took cargoes of up to 100,000 skins a trip. In 1806 Joseph Banks' secretary noted: "The island of Van Diemen, the southwest coast of New Holland . . . produce seals of all kinds in quantities at present almost innumerable. The beach is encumbered with their quantities and those who visit their haunts have less trouble in killing them than the servants of the victuallers have who kill hogs in a pound . . ."

But before the first decade was ended, the seal population of Bass Strait was drastically diminished. The great ships departed for more profitable places, leaving the islands to a few vagabond vessels, to members of sealing gangs placed on the islands who chose to remain and make their homes there, to runaways from ships and convict settlements. From these

Original church, old settlement, Flinders Island, is now a shearing shed. It should be restored by National Trust.

Sooty petrels (mutton birds) feed by the thousand near Flinders Island. Mutton birding is a major industry on the island, and Lady Barron, in the south, is the centre for preservation.

Coprosma repens, the orange-berried taupata of New Zealand, is naturalized on the islands of Bass Strait.

Pink-flowered form of Epacris impressa, *blooming on Vinegar Hill near Lady Barron, Flinders Island.*

Flower spike of the silver banksia, Banksia marginata, *in bud, March.*

adventurers and their native consorts, kidnapped from Tasmania and the mainland (for when the sealers came to Bass Strait, no native peoples lived on the islands), sprang a colourful, distinctive group known as the Straitsmen. They lived by hunting, fishing, tending small crops, sealing and mutton-birding in season and, it is said, occasionally reaping a sea-harvest from wrecked ships. In the eighteen-thirties they were joined by the tragic remnants of the Tasmanian Aborigines, exiled to Flinders Island in the Furneaux Group after the Black War which reduced their numbers to less than two hundred. For generations these island people lived in isolation. Then, in the face of increasing settlement and an influx of outsiders, they drifted from their home islands and congregated on the western end of Cape Barren Island; the old name, Straitsmen, lost currency and they came to be known as Cape Barren Islanders. In recent years another turn of the wheel has brought greater opportunities than those provided on the limited area of land reserved for them on Cape Barren; they are leaving their isolation and reclaiming their lost islands. Today's cray fishers and moon-birders are the descendants of the strangely assorted settlers of last century.

Dairying, beef cattle and sheep farming are now the major occupations on King Island, once the abode of huge sea elephants and the dread of Bass Strait mariners, who feared its sharp rocks and sudden storms. This island at the western end of Bass Strait is the graveyard of many ships.

Cattle walk over the graves of drowned sailors, Cape Wickham. Many King Islanders are descendants of shipwreck survivors.

Seal Rocks, King Island, where fur seals once congregated in thousands.

In January, 1801, John Black, captain of the brig *Harbinger* out of Capetown with a cargo of rum and wines for the settlement at Port Jackson, sighted an island at the western mouth of Bass Strait and named it for the newly installed Governor Philip Gidley King. He was not, however, the discoverer of King Island for that honour belongs to a sealing captain, Reid of the *Martha,* who reported its existence in 1798. The island remained unaffected by sighting or naming until 1802, a hectic year so far as European contact was concerned. In January, John Murray in *Lady Nelson* charted the eastern coastline. Sealers visited it – one, Campbell of the *Harrington,* reported finding wreckage of an unknown ship there in March; he picked up a cat, the only survivor. In April, Flinders in *Investigator* passed under its lee, and in December the island was the scene of a comic opera flag-hoisting, which came about this way: French navigator Nicolas Baudin, commissioned by the Institut de France to explore the southern seas in the cause of science, called on Governor King at Sydney Cove before sailing for Bass Strait. No sooner had he left than King, the cautious, worried by rumours of French plans for a colony in Van Diemen's Land, sent a Lieutenant Robbins after Baudin to warn him of British claims to the area. Meeting up with Baudin at Sea Elephant Bay, King Island, the eager and over-zealous Robbins hastily hoisted the flag over the French tents, solemnly saluted it, fired a volley over the heads of the bewildered Frenchmen, and formally took possession in the name of the King – a somewhat redundant ceremony since the island had been officially British for two years!

Then came the Bass Strait rush for furs and oil. The island earned a grim reputation as a graveyard of ships – sixty were lost there in half a century, with a death-toll of over two thousand lives. More than two hundred – mostly convict women and children – were drowned when the transport *Neva* was wrecked in 1835. Ten years later the emigrant ship *Cataraqui,* bound for Melbourne, went down with a loss of over four hundred lives; 314 of the victims lie buried in five graves. There were only nine survivors, who were rescued by sealers after some days without food or adequate clothing. Today, King Island presents a face of rural tranquility. Cattle graze over the graves of the drowned; descendants of shipwreck survivors tend the green fields.

Sheep graze on rich pastures, King Island, Bass Strait.

Trees are planted as wind breaks around farm houses, Sea Elephant Bay.

Native pigface (Carpobrotus species) scrambles over the sandy hind dunes.

ISLANDS OF BASS STRAIT

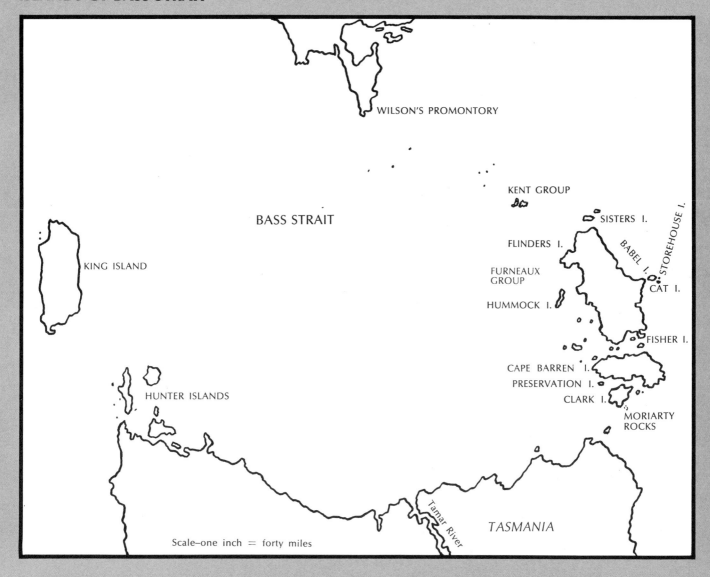

WILSON'S PROMONTORY

KENT GROUP

BASS STRAIT

SISTERS I.

STOREHOUSE I.

FLINDERS I.

BABEL I.

KING ISLAND

FURNEAUX
GROUP

CAT I.

HUMMOCK I.

FISHER I.

HUNTER ISLANDS

CAPE BARREN I.

PRESERVATION I.

CLARK I.

MORIARTY
ROCKS

Tamar River

TASMANIA

Scale—one inch = forty miles

TASMANIA & ADJACENT ISLANDS

Powder magazine at Port Arthur, built in the eighteen-thirties. Port Arthur, infamous penal settlement on sea-locked Tasman Peninsula, locale last century of unparalleled anguish and cruelty, consists of freestone buildings of singular beauty (convict architect James Blackburn was designer of the church) in a setting of natural grandeur. The huge sea cave pictured opposite is near Port Arthur.

Tasmania is a mountainous island. Almost half the total area is above 2,000 feet, and the highlands are dominated by spectacular residual peaks and ranges, 5,000 feet or more high – Cradle Mountain, Barn Bluff, Ben Lomond, Mount Pelion and Mount Ossa. The great glacier-scoured central plateau, stony and virtually treeless, is a place of awesome grandeur, a land of lakes gouged by the retreating ice age. The northern margin of the tableland is the highest. Here the Western Tiers, mighty fault escarpment, rise abruptly from the coastal lowlands – a great wall facing Bass Strait, almost uniformly high (4,000 feet), straight and unbroken except where cleft by the northward-flowing rivers which plunge seaward through deep, almost parallel gorges. Southward the slope is gradual, a giant tilted tableland dissected by numerous rivers fed by glacial lakes. Lake St Clair, the Great Lake, Lake Echo, Lake Sorell – all drain southeast into the valley of the Derwent, the great river complex which roughly bisects the major portion of Tasmania. To the west lies a wilderness of mist-shrouded mountains and rain-drenched gorges; to the east the grassy plains of the Midlands, Tasmania's major sheep-grazing area, extend to the Eastern Tiers and the fertile, heavily timbered coastal strip.

Much of Tasmania is composed of dolerite, a dark, coarse-grained rock of volcanic origin formed when molten lava was forced upwards and then sideways, intruding horizontally into sandstone stratas laid down in Triassic times when much of the island was covered with a vast freshwater lake. This rock is the basis of Tasmania's durable tableland and spectacular mountain and coastal scenery. Great sheets of dolerite, lying one above the other, form most of the high land; the sandstone stratas which they invaded have long since worn away, or remain only as isolated islands embedded in a stony sea. Tasmania's highest mountains are composed of dolerite, and her glacier-gouged lakes are ringed with black dolerite cliffs, often rising sheer for hundreds of feet above the deep still waters, sometimes as isolated square-sided pillars – for a remarkable feature of dolerite is its columnar construction which causes it to weather into spectacular hexagonal columns. This is most noticeable on the sea coast, where the rock formations face the full force of winds from Antarctica. Cape Raoul and Cape Pillar, on the most southerly points of Tasman Peninsula, are composed of lofty dolerite cliffs, columns closely packed into jagged groups or isolated against the skyline as slender pillars hundreds of feet high (those at Cape Raoul are known as the Organ Pipes). Fluted Cape, which marks the southern end of Adventure Bay, Bruny Island – described by Tobias Furneaux in 1773 as "a high bluff point, the rocks whereof were like so many fluted pillars" – is another example, and similar formations occur at South West Cape, Tasmania's most southerly point. These dolerite formations, however, do not extend to the west and southwest; that wild and rugged area, oldest land surface in the island, is composed of ancient schists and quartzite rocks.

*Hobart, on the Derwent River at the foot
of Mount Wellington, is the second oldest
city in Australia, settled in 1804.*

*The lighthouse on Low Head, which
marks the entrance to the Tamar River,
was built with convict labour in 1833 and
was for some time manned by convicts.*

*Cloud-shrouded Mount Wellington,
4000-odd feet high, rises abruptly from
the banks of the Derwent River.*

Abel Janzoon Tasman was the first European known
to sight the island which now bears his name. On
24th November, 1642, his ship, *Zeehaen*, made
landfall near the present Cape Sorell, midpoint of
the rugged west coast at the entrance to Macquarie
Harbour. Tasman named his discovery Anthony
Van Diemen's Land in honour of the Governor-
General of the Dutch East Indies who had
commissioned the voyage, and this remained the
official name until 1855 though, by then, it had
popularly been supplanted by "Tasmania" for many
years. Following the coastline southward, Tasman
rounded South West Cape, sighted and named
Maatsuker and other outlying islands, and
continued eastward to the bay he named Stormy –
after he had been driven out to sea by a fierce
northwest gale. Tasman Peninsula was rounded on
1st December, and the following day the ships
anchored in Marion Bay, where a party landed and
explored the country. The next day Tasman took
formal possession of Van Diemen's Land for
Holland; the seas were too rough to land a boat, but
the ship's carpenter, Pieter Jacobzoon, swam ashore
and raised the Dutch flag. Continuing northward,
Tasman sighted and named Maria Island (after Van
Diemen's wife) and Scouten Island.

The next white contact was more than a century later,
when French navigator Captain Nicholas Marion du
Fresne, in 1772, followed Tasman's track around the
southern portion of the island, anchoring also in
the bay which now bears his name; the party spent
six days there. Marion was followed in 1773 by
Tobias Furneaux, in command of Cook's companion
ship *Adventure,* who made landfall near South West
Cape, spent some days at Adventure Bay, Bruny
Island (though he remained unaware that he
had not, in fact, landed on the mainland) and
skirted the east coast to Eddystone Point and the
Bass Strait island group which now bears his name.
Cook himself visited Adventure Bay during his third
voyage, on 26th January, 1777, anchoring for several
days to take on wood, water and supplies of
greenstuff for the cattle he had aboard. Master of
Resolution on that voyage was one William Bligh,
then 21 years old; as captain of the *Bounty,* he
anchored in Adventure Bay again in 1788, on his
way to Tahiti and mutiny, and returned once more
in 1792, when he carried out surveys on H.M.S.
Providence. (Bligh was later to re-visit the area after
another mutiny: in 1809, after he had been deposed
as Governor of New South Wales by Major
Johnson and the Rum Corps, he sailed *Porpoise* to
the new settlement at Hobart, and stationed the
vessel for some months in Storm Bay.)
Further French expeditions followed the British
sailors. In 1793 Bruni d'Entrecasteaux in *La*

Tasmanian devil, Sarcophilus harrisii, *a small carnivorous marsupial found only in Tasmania; fossils indicate it once occurred also on the mainland.*

This huge whale is being torn to pieces by a pack of killer sharks. It is a blue-backed whale, largest mammal the world has ever known, which grows to a hundred or more feet.

Tasmanian masked owl, Tyto castanops *(also called the chestnut-faced owl), occurs only in Tasmania but is related to the masked owl of the mainland.*

Sugar glider, Petaurus breviceps, *widespread in eastern States, is recorded as having been introduced to Tasmania in 1835 but its wide distribution there suggests it is possibly indigenous.*

Tasmanian pademelon, Thyogale billardierii, *is abundant in Tasmania, and occurs also in Victoria.*

Recherche, with Huon de Kermadec in *L'Esperance,* on a voyage in search of the lost La Pérouse, explored part of the southern coast in detail, charting and naming Recherche Bay, Port Esperance and the entrance to the Huon River, sailing through d'Entrecasteaux Channel and for the first time establishing the insularity of Bruny Island. Two months later English captain John Hayes unknowingly followed in their footsteps, bestowing English names on landmarks lately named by the French; Hayes charted and named the Derwent River and Risdon Cove, original site of Hobart. In 1798 Bass and Flinders, sailing from Sydney Cove, navigated Bass Strait and made the first circumnavigation of Tasmania, and in 1803 Governor King, spurred by the activities of the French expedition led by Nicolas Baudin – and also the needs of the booming Bass Strait sealing trade – ordered the establishment of a settlement on the Derwent. The following year he sent a party of settlers and convicts to Georgetown, on Port Dalrymple at the mouth of the Tamar (two years later this settlement was moved upstream to the site of the present city of Launceston.)

And so Van Diemen's Land left its dreamtime. For the first decade the two settlements – north and south – were under separate government, following individual paths: a curious omen for the future, not of the settlements but of the settlers. On the one hand, a liberal policy of land grants, assigned convict labour, and loans based on capital led to the establishment of a landed gentry aping that of England. Hawthorn hedges clambered over the alien island. Magnificent colonial mansions mimicked the stately homes of England. Elm and oak, ash and poplar, jostled the eucalypts aside, shedding flamboyant autumn leaves, carving a piece of England from the sombre countryside. On the other hand, Van Diemen's Land became the gaol of Britain and the sister-colony, a dreaded place of secondary punishment penal settlements. Macquarie Harbour on the west coast was the first site selected in 1821. Accessible only by sea, through a narrow strait appropriately named Hell's Gates, hemmed in by formidable mountains, it was regarded as remote enough to deter escape.

39

The only known examples of the art of the Tasmanian Aborigines are pecked intaglios; most, like these at Mount Cameron West, are variations of circles and ovals, combined with rows of indentations which appear to have been gradually deepened over centuries. The Tasmanians did not long survive the impact of white civilization; they are now extinct, victims of the only instance of successful genocide in recorded history. The first shots in the so-called Black War were fired in the first months of the first settlement, at Risdon Cove in May 1804. This set the pattern: sealers stole their women; settlers seized their hunting grounds and shot them on sight. The last shots rang out in the eighteen-thirties, during Governor Arthur's farcical "Black Line" round-up of the tragic remains of an ancient race.

Canoe tree, Lake St Clair. The story of the lost Tasmanians can still be traced on the rocks and trees of the island.

The Organ Pipes at Cape Raoul on the southern tip of Tasman Peninsula are composed of dolerite, a dark columnar rock of volcanic origin. Great waves from the southern ocean have eroded these cliffs into a series of regular, vertical hexagonal columns, sometimes packed closely together, sometimes isolated as slender pillars hundreds of feet high.

The hulk in the foreground is the barque Otago, commanded by Joseph Conrad on his third visit to Australia in 1887. This famous ship now lies rotting in the Derwent River, within sight of Hobart and overlooked by Mount Wellington.

Autumn in the valley of the Derwent.

Tree-ferns, Dicksonia antarctica, *near Russell Falls, Mount Field National Park.*

Old mill at Oatlands, built in 1837. Martin Cash the bushranger operated in this area, ranging the highway between Hobart and Launceston.

Tasman Island, off Cape Pillar, Tasman Peninsula, is separated from the mainland by a shallow, mile-wide strait.

Coles Bay, Freycinet Peninsula; the ketch Lauriana *is in the foreground.*

Nevertheless, conditions there were so harsh that many attempted to do so, some successfully. One such was Matthew Brady; in June, 1824, with others, he stole a boat and escaped by sea to South Arm Others attempted escape by land, the most notorious being Alexander Pierce, the original of Marcus Clarke's Mat Gabbett in *For the Term of His Natural Life.* In 1822 he left with eight companions; only he survived, reputedly having murdered and eaten the others. For some time he operated as a lone bushranger, plundering isolated settlements, but was eventually recaptured and returned to Macquarie Harbour. A group of convicts seized the transport *Cyprus,* on its way to Macquarie Harbour from Hobart in 1829. They sailed it to Japan, where some left; others returned to England, and a number were recaptured and sent back to Van Diemen's Land. But though the convicts continued to "bolt" from their remote gaol, the factor of isolation which led to its selection made communication so difficult that Governor Arthur decided to move the settlement to Tasman's Peninsula. Building of Port Arthur began in 1830, and in 1833 Macquarie Harbour was abandoned. The final round went to the convicts: in January, 1834, after the main party had left, a group of eleven seized the brig *Frederick,* then on the stocks, and made off for Chile. Four were later recaptured there; the others escaped. From bolters to bushrangers is a logical step, and Van Diemen's Land, gaol of the twice-convicted, produced some of the most violent, and also some of the boldest and most daring. Matthew Brady, mentioned above, stormed the township of Sorell, captured the soldiers sent to search for him, and locked them in the town gaol after first releasing other prisoners. Michael Howe impudently corresponded with Sorell, Lieutenant-Governor of the day, as "governor of the ranges" to "governor of the town." This man was the subject of the first book published in Tasmania, a biography titled, somewhat optimistically, *Michael Howe, the Last and Worst of the Bushrangers of Van Dieman's Land.* It was published in 1818, a few months after his death. Martin Cash, one of the few who avoided a violent end and finished life as a respectable citizen, escaped twice from Port Arthur, swimming along Eaglehawk Neck, the narrow isthmus closely guarded by fierce dogs tethered only inches apart. He built a fortress on Mount Dromedary, 20-odd miles from Hobart, and carried out a series of daring raids over an extensive area. Captured and sent to Norfolk Island, he became a model prisoner and was pardoned after a few years. Cash was one of the first to make respectable capital out of wrongdoing; his autobiography, published in 1870, ran into many editions.

Left: Keeper checks light on windswept Cape Bruny. Below: Spiral stairway in the historic building. This lighthouse, on the southern shore of Bruny Island, is one of the oldest in Tasmania. It was built in 1836 with convict labour, following shipping disasters in D'Entrecasteaux Channel; the convict transport George III and the migrant ship Enchantress, were wrecked within weeks of each other in 1835, at a cost of one hundred and eighty-four lives.

TASMANIA AND ADJACENT ISLANDS

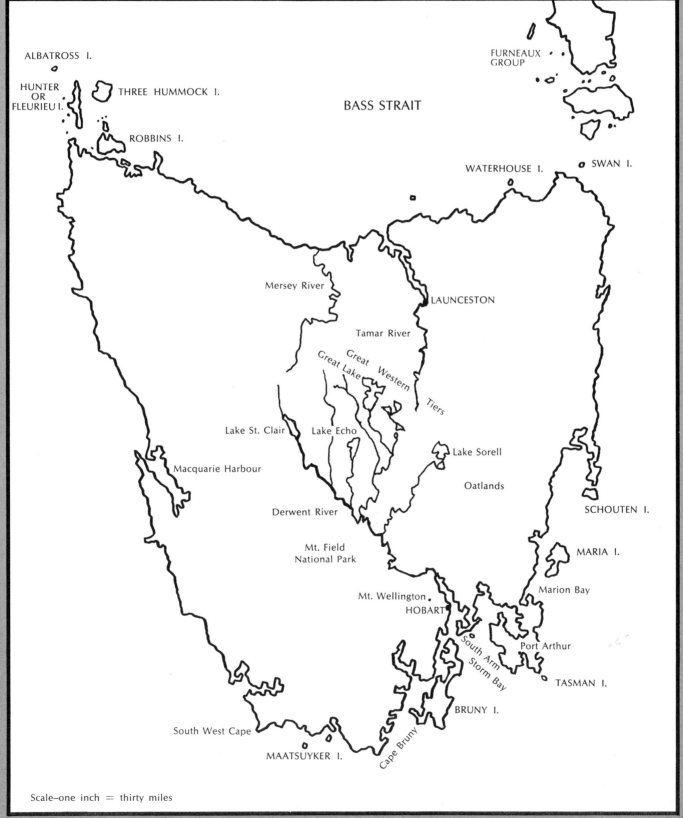

ALBATROSS I.

FURNEAUX GROUP

HUNTER OR FLEURIEU I.

THREE HUMMOCK I.

BASS STRAIT

ROBBINS I.

WATERHOUSE I.

SWAN I.

Mersey River

LAUNCESTON

Tamar River

Great Western Tiers

Great Lake

Lake St. Clair

Lake Echo

Lake Sorell

Macquarie Harbour

Oatlands

SCHOUTEN I.

Derwent River

MARIA I.

Mt. Field National Park

Marion Bay

Mt. Wellington

HOBART

South Arm

Port Arthur

Storm Bay

TASMAN I.

BRUNY I.

South West Cape

Cape Bruny

MAATSUYKER I.

Scale—one inch = thirty miles

Phillip Island · The Twelve Apostles · Kangaroo Island
Wedge Island · Recherche Archipelago

ISLANDS OF THE
SOUTHERN SEAS

The Twelve Apostles, near Port Campbell, Victoria, are residual sandstone stacks carved from the coastline by the sea.

Kangaroo Island is a drowned mountain, isolated by rising seas of the last ice age. Composed mainly of granite, overlaid by ancient marine limestones, it faces the full force of winds from Antarctica.

The off-shore islands of Australia's southern coast are remnants of a drowned continent, isolated by rising seas or carved from the coastline by winds and waves from Antarctica. Some are large, rugged and mountainous; others are mere specks, isolated rocky peaks of ancient hills rising abruptly from the stormy seas or wave-worn to dangerous reefs, awash at high tide. There are also islands in the making, high promontories linked to the land by a low isthmus. These mountain-islands are composed of granite, outriders of the mainland defying the ocean, but in places along the southern coast, where land which was formerly beneath the sea has been elevated and the coastline consists of sedimentary rocks, there are islands of sandstone, will-o'-the-wisp islands that chop and change as the sea cuts and carves the coastline, leaving the slightly harder rocks isolated as off-shore stacks. Always the sea is master, making and breaking the land.

Gabo is a granite island, the most easterly off the southern coast. It is separated from the mainland by a shallow channel, and its lighthouse marks the turning point of the sea lanes along the south and east coast of Australia. Westward along the Victorian coast is Wilson's Promontory, most southerly point of the mainland, a mighty granite bastion jutting out into Bass Strait, which George Bass, its discoverer, described as "a cornerstone of this great island, New Holland." Wilson's Promontory is a mountainous peninsula, the northern portion of the great land bridge which once linked Tasmania to the mainland, and it is surrounded by the drowned peaks of that former high ridge. Largest is Snake Island; it lies across the mouth of Corner Inlet, protecting the isthmus of Wilson's Promontory and sheltering the fishing port of Welshpool, once a haven for the oldtime whalers and now a major centre of Bass Strait fishermen. There are numerous smaller islands. Most spectacular is probably Rodondo, a sheer peak of red granite rising 1500 feet above the sea, just off the tip of the promontory. Apart from seabird visitors, only insects inhabit this bare island.

From Wilson's Promontory the southern coastline veers northward to the broad inlet of Western Port, where there are two large islands, Phillip at the entrance and French Island in the centre, the latter so named because of visits to it by the French scientific expedition led by Nicolas Baudin in 1802. (A later visit by the French – Dumont D'Urville on *Astrolabe* in 1826 – led to revival of earlier fears of French colonisation and the second attempt at settlement on Australia's southern shores: a military and convict establishment at Phillip Island, abandoned within a week owing to scarcity of drinking water.) Phillip Island was first sighted by Bass in 1798; he described it as having "a high cape, like a snapper's head," and it was known as Snapper Island until later officially named for Governor Phillip. A tiny islet off the northeast corner of Phillip Island was the site of the first attempt at cultivation in Victoria; James Grant, visiting the area on *Lady Nelson* in 1801, planted seeds of various vegetables and grains, and later the

Admiral's Arch, Kangaroo Island.
Waves of the southern ocean have
penetrated a huge limestone cave.

Historic ruins near Cape Couedic.

The Dinosaur, one of many strange
weather-worn rocks on Kangaroo Island.

Phillip Island is a sanctuary for the
fairy penguin, Eudyptula minor.

Wedge Island, at mouth of Spencer Gulf.

same year John Murray found the little plantation thriving, the wheat six feet high "with stalks like young sugar cane." Today Phillip Island is a tourist resort with the emphasis on conservation. Koalas taken there for sanctuary after the wholesale slaughter in the first quarter of this century have flourished to such an extent that the mainland has been substantially restocked from their numbers. Along the seaward coastline there are several muttonbird rookeries, and a colony of seals inhabits off-shore rocks. But the main feature of Phillip Island is the fairy penguins, which take over the southwest corner of the island during the nesting season, from September to March. These quaint little birds are the smallest of the penguins, and the only members of the group to make their home in Australian waters. They are rather comical on land, waddling along the beach in regimented rows, heads craned forward and flipper-wings extended as balancers, but in the water they are swift and graceful. Unlike other water birds, they do not use their webbed feet as propellors, but fly beneath the sea's surface on modified wings. Fantastic sandstone islands, in all stages of disintegration, occur off the Victorian coast on the western side of the Otway Peninsula. Some are hollowed into series of natural bridges, others have been reduced to ragged lines of residual stacks. Further westward the old granite hills march once more into the sea. Kangaroo Island, which lies across the Gulf of St. Vincent in South Australia, is geologically the southern extremity of the Mount Lofty Ranges, sea-severed from the tip of Fleurieu Peninsula by a deep and narrow passage called the Backstairs. It is composed mainly of granite, overlaid by ancient marine limestones, which winds and waves from Antarctica have wrought into many strange, fantastic shapes. Matthew Flinders discovered Kangaroo Island in 1802; he and his crew feasted on fresh kangaroo flesh, and the island was named in honour of the event. The animal they shot there – thirty-one on the first day – was the Kangaroo Island kangaroo, a sooty-brown insular form of the mainland forester or great grey kangaroo. It is still common on the island, as is the Kangaroo Island wallaby, an insular subspecies of the tammar wallaby, but the little Kangaroo Island emu, described by Flinders and also by Baudin and his naturalists, was extinct by the time of the first official attempt at settlement in 1836. This was soon abandoned in favour of the present site of Adelaide, but the island was earlier occupied by a colony of sealers, whalers and runaway convicts, who were probably largely responsible for the extermination of the emu. The American brig *Union* was first on the scene, in 1803; in June, 1804, she landed at Sydney a record haul of 14,000 sealskins. While on the island, the crew built and launched a thirty-five ton vessel, in a sheltered arm of the sea now called American River. In the following years this island became headquarters for sealers working the southern coast, reputedly a wild and lawless lot who, like their counterparts in Bass Strait, raided Tasmania and the mainland for native wives. The last of the Tasmanian Aborigines was a woman carried to Kangaroo Island by sealers. She died there in 1888.

London Bridge, one of many curious islets in the making, near Port Campbell.

The Archipelago of the Recherche, near Port Esperance, Western Australia, is a maze of islands and shoals stretching for more than a hundred miles at the western extremity of the Great Australian Bight. First recorded by D'Entrecasteaux in 1792 and named for one of his ships, it is the home of the unique Recherche rock wallaby, Petrogale hacketti, an insular species. On the Investigator Group at the eastern end of the Bight is another distinctive but closely related species, the Pearson Island rock wallaby, P. pearsoni.

ISLANDS OF THE SOUTHERN SEAS

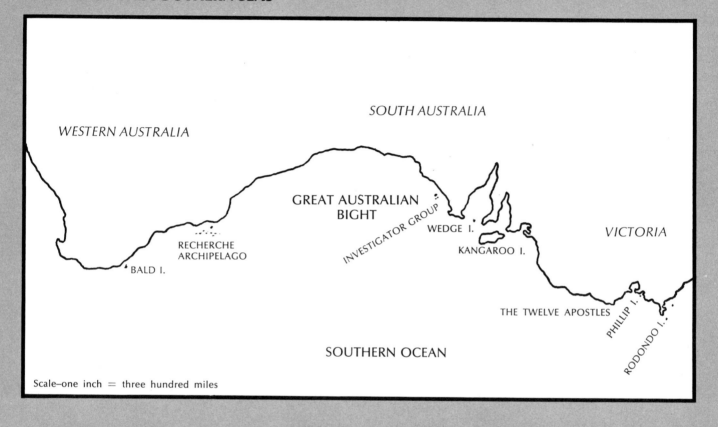

Rottnest Island   ·   Houtman Abrolhos   ·   Dirk Hartog Island
Barrow Island   ·   Buccaneer Archipelago
Cockatoo Island

ISLANDS OF THE WEST

These are the treasure islands of Australia's western main. Traditional treasure of coin and bullion, and the twentieth century treasure of oil and iron, lie beneath the sea and sand. There is also another treasure, threatened and irreplaceable, on these numerous scattered isles: a unique wildlife, evolved and preserved by countless centuries of isolation.
They are harsh, these golden islands of the west, many of them waterless, most of them surrounded by dangerous seas and treacherous reefs, and their history, since the first white contact, is equally harsh – a tale of murder and shipwreck, mutiny and buried treasure, death by gun and gibbet, sea and sword, of men marooned to fend alone in an alien and unknown land. Dutch mariners, bound for Batavia and the spice islands of the East Indies, were the first Europeans known to sail these waters. Abandoning the old Portuguese seaway along the African coast to India, they sailed instead directly eastward across the Southern Ocean until near the meridian of their destination, borne by such steady and favourable winds that the journey, though longer in miles, was shorter by months. Inevitably those same steady winds carried them closer to the coast of Australia; navigation aids of the early seventeenth century were supplemented largely by guesswork, and those who overran the meridian of Batavia were wont to sight ahead of them the dim outline of an unknown coast, a forbidding, reef-stewn, rocky coast which claimed many of their vessels, some doubtless unrecorded. Dirck Hartog, on *Eendracht,* was the first to bring back a description of the country. In 1616 he made landfall and left a record of his visit on a pewter plate.

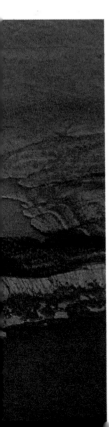

Drilling for oil, Barrow Island. This island is the home of several unique species of native mammals, and early this century was proclaimed a class A reserve for the protection of fauna and flora. Such reserves however are not exempted from the Mining Act, and development of the area as a big oil-producing centre has threatened the continued existence of the island's wildlife.

They fish the waters of Australia's most westerly islands: fishermen unloading a catch at Shark Bay, inlet bounded by the islands of Dirk Hartog, Dorre and Bernier.

The Buccaneer Archipelago, named for English buccaneer William Dampier who sailed among its countless islands in 1688. These islands of iron rival in dramatic beauty the better-known tropical islands of the Whitsunday Passage, on the other side of the continent.

Pink-flowered member of the Brachychiton paradoxum group, photographed on Cockatoo Island, Yampi Sound. This wildflower grows right across the top of tropical Australia.

Quokka or short-tailed padmelon, Setonix brachyurus. Rottnest Island owes its name to this quaint little marsupial; in 1696 Dutch mariner de Vlamingh, deceived by their tiny size and short hindlimbs, named their home "Rotte Nest" (Rat's Nest). He described the island as a "terrestrial paradise . .". Below, one of the many lovely sheltered bays that scallop the coastline.

Marine archaelogist searches the coral reefs and limestone sea caves of Houtmans Abrolhos for relics from the Batavia.

The wreck of the Batavia was followed by mutiny and murder; this bullet, recovered recently, was lodged in a human skull.

Bronze cannon from the Batavia, recovered in 1963; it is in perfect condition.

A simple pile of stones of great historic significance: the crude fort built as defence against the onslaughts of the mutineers.

The rough charts the Dutch drew of the new-found Great South Land named this island Dirck Hartog's Ree (safe anchorage), and hopes were held that Marco Polo's fabled beach of gold and spices might yet be found. Their mariners probed its coast, scattering Dutch names on prominent landmarks, only to be repulsed by this ancient, arid land. Frederik de Houtman was the next of any note; he sighted, but did not land on, Rottnest Island, then proceeded northward for two days until, unexpectedly and before dawn, he came among the reefs and islands now known as Houtmans Abrolhos (a term which, translated roughly, means "open your eyes"). These coral and limestone islands lie towards the edge of the continental shelf, in three groups roughly parallel to the coast and forty miles away. Scene of many shipwrecks, they amply justify their warning name. First and most notorious was the wreck of the *Batavia,* which struck a reef in the northern Wallabi Group in 1629. *Batavia,* commanded by Francois Pelsaert, carried about 300 crew and passengers (mainly migrants to the East Indies) and eleven chests of money. Forty people were drowned, but the others reached two small islands. These proved to be waterless, and after a week's vain search on nearby islands and the mainland, Pelsaert headed for Batavia to summon help. With him were forty-five men, two women and a baby; all survived the journey, which was completed in thirty days, and a week later, Pelsaert set out again to rescue the castaways. Meanwhile, on the island aptly named Batavia's Graveyard, an incredible tale of massacre and mutiny was unfolding. Supercargo Jerome Cornelius took command, decided to solve the problem of shortage of food and water by murdering most of the survivors, and, with a

The tough and hardy folk of Shark Bay and
adjacent islands are in many cases the
descendants of early pearlers; their
faces often show a mixture of many races,
always reflect the harsh climate.
Below: Wool from historic Dirk Hartog
Island, now a sheep station, fenced by sea.

Replica of Dirk Hartog's Plate.

Sturt's desert pea Clianthus formosa,
grows on the islands; Dampier gathered
the first specimens here in 1699.

Replica of the Dirk Hartog Plate
The original of this plate (now in the
National Museum, Amsterdam) was
nailed to a post on Dirk Hartog Island,
Shark Bay by Dirk Hartog, Captain
of the ship "Eendracht" in 1616. The plate
was to commemorate his landing and it
remained until it was discovered by
Captain Vlamingh in 1697. Vlamingh removed the plate and took it to Batavia
(now Djakarta) Eventually the plate was
sent back to Holland.

chosen few, to seize the rescue ship when it arrived and use it for pirating, with *Batavia's* money chests his first prize. At first the murders were surreptitious; men were seized by night and drowned at sea, and their absence explained by a tale that they had been taken to other islands. Then came open massacre. The pirates assumed complete control, sparing only those who signed an oath of allegiance. Cornelius and his lieutenants paraded in gaudy gold-braided clothes looted from *Batavia's* treasure chests. Men and children were murdered, women occasionally spared and shared. But on one island, called High Island (probably West Wallabi) there was still a group of people sent there earlier by Cornelius to search for water. This party, under the leadership of a soldier, Webbye Hayes, found water – and at the same time heard of the murders from survivors who escaped the slaughter. Barricades were built, and weapons – crude pikes and clubs – hastily constructed. They drove off two attacks, and captured Cornelius in the third. The mutineers were launching a final attack when Pelsaert appeared in the rescue ship. After a frantic race in rowboats, Hayes succeeded in warning him of the situation, and the remaining pirates were captured. But the tale of human woe and anguish on the islands of Houtmans Abrolhos did not end there. Not even with the torture and execution of most of the mutineers on the first gibbets erected in Australia, and the marooning on the mainland of two considered to be less culpable – never to be heard of again, though mariners sought for them over many years. (Legend points to light-skinned Aborigines and suggests they were descendants of marooned Dutchmen.) One hundred and twenty-five were murdered from *Batavia,* forty were drowned and eight were hung; over the centuries that followed they were joined by others, and there is scarcely an island or reef in the group that is not marked by shipwreck and its aftermath. Survivors from the *Zeewyck,* wrecked in the Pelsaert Group in 1726, have left many traces of their stay. They spent almost a year on the islands, existing on seals and muttonbirds, and rainwater trapped in limestone caverns. From the wreckage of their ship they built the first vessel constructed by white men in Australia; a small sloop which they successfully sailed to Batavia, complete with *Zeewyck's* money chests.

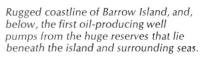
Rugged coastline of Barrow Island, and, below, the first oil-producing well pumps from the huge reserves that lie beneath the island and surrounding seas.

Wildflowers of Barrow Island, blooming in August. The hibiscus-like pink flower is Gossypium robinsonii, which grows only in a limited area of the north west coast and some adjacent islands. Below is a mulla mulla, Ptilotus obovatus, a low shrub with silvery-grey woolly leaves.

Acacia *species (wattles) and* Pimelea
species, growing on Barrow Island.

The pied oyster-catcher, Haematopus
ostralegus, *was featured in the first
published pictures of Australian birds —
in Dampier's account of his second voyage
to Australia, in 1699.*

The Barrow Island wallaby, Lagorchestes
conspicillatus, *is found only on the
island. It is used as a bait for fish traps as
witnessed by the author.*

The Buccaneer Archipelago, Yampi Sound
— bay of a thousand islands. Fantastically
beautiful in all moods, they are nevertheless harsh islands, islands of iron ringed by
stark colourful cliffs and surrounded by
the most dangerous seas of the west coast,
where great tides create violent rips
and treacherous whirlpools. The many art
galleries on Cockatoo Island (below) and
other islands of the group indicate that in
the past they knew Aboriginal life, though
most have no natural water.

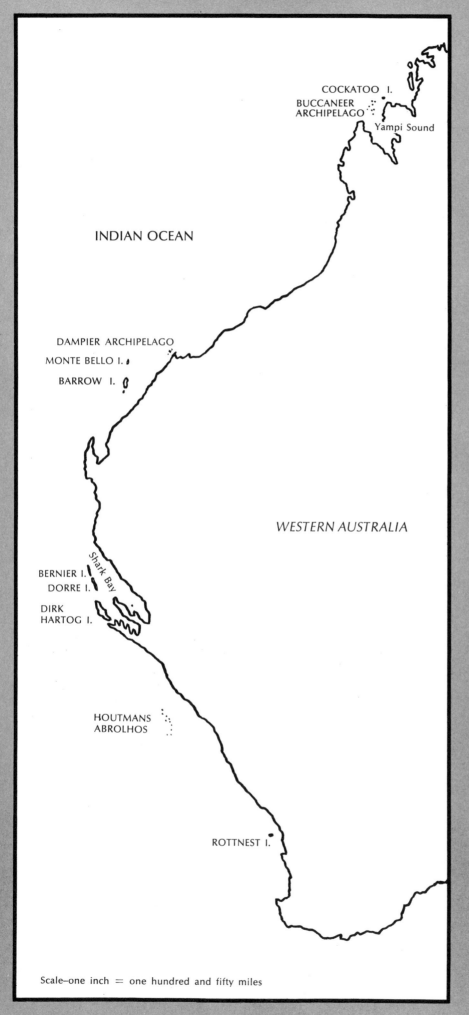

ISLANDS OF THE WEST

COCKATOO I.
BUCCANEER
ARCHIPELAGO
Yampi Sound

INDIAN OCEAN

DAMPIER ARCHIPELAGO
MONTE BELLO I.
BARROW I.

WESTERN AUSTRALIA

BERNIER I. Shark Bay
DORRE I.
DIRK
HARTOG I.

HOUTMANS
ABROLHOS

ROTTNEST I.

Scale—one inch = one hundred and fifty miles

ISLANDS OF ARNHEM LAND

*Trees and cycads (probably Cycas media)
growing on Bathurst Island. These islands
of the north once formed part of the
old land bridge to Timor. Vegetation is
lush and tropical with a strong
Indo-Malaysian element.*

*Corroboree man, Elcho Island. Aborigines
still follow their traditional way of life on
many of the islands of Arnhem Land.*

The first Australians are believed to have come to this country across
the island bridges of the shallow Arafura Sea which borders Arnhem Land.
They came from Ceylon and southern Asia, countless centuries ago, and
from these islands drifted across the continent, claiming it for their own
in the most intimate way; every part of it had personality for them,
every rock, every tree, had a name and a story. Now their time has
come round again, and the islands of Arnhem Land – the ancient link, the
umbilical cord of an age-old culture – are today among the last remaining
outposts of the world of the first Australians. In the isolation of these
islands they still in most respects follow their traditional life,
although, paradoxically, these are the people who have experienced
the most alien contact, dating back over many centuries. Perhaps it is
this very factor which has enabled them to cope with changes from
outside, to adjust to conflicting concepts.

Arnhem Land mythology echoes this alien-orientation. All their creative
beings came from the sea – the Djanggawul sisters and brother, who
followed the morning star from their mother, the sun, paddling a bark
canoe until they arrived at eastern Arnhem Land and its islands;
Laindjung-Banaidja, the father-son pair who could assume female form
at will, rose from the sea in the same area, bodies bearing variegated
watermarks preserved today as totemic patterns. In the west the fertility
mother, Waramurunggoindju, and her husband, Wuraggag, are said
to have come from Macassar, the faraway island (Celebes) over the
sea, and other ancestral and spirit beings of the region are also
alleged to have come out of the sea, from some far distant place to
the northwest. This was in the beginning, the dreamtime. Between then
and February, 1803, when Matthew Flinders reported seeing Macassan
praus in the "Malay Road" near Elcho Island, the islanders of Arnhem
Land knew many foreign contacts. Their songs record the visits of the
Baijini people, pre-Macassans who came also from the western
islands beyond the Arafura and Timor Seas. They sing of the ships in
which these people came, of their women who wove cloth and
cultivated gardens, of the stone houses they built and their golden skin,
lighter than that of the Macassans. Indeed, the Baijini era is drifting into

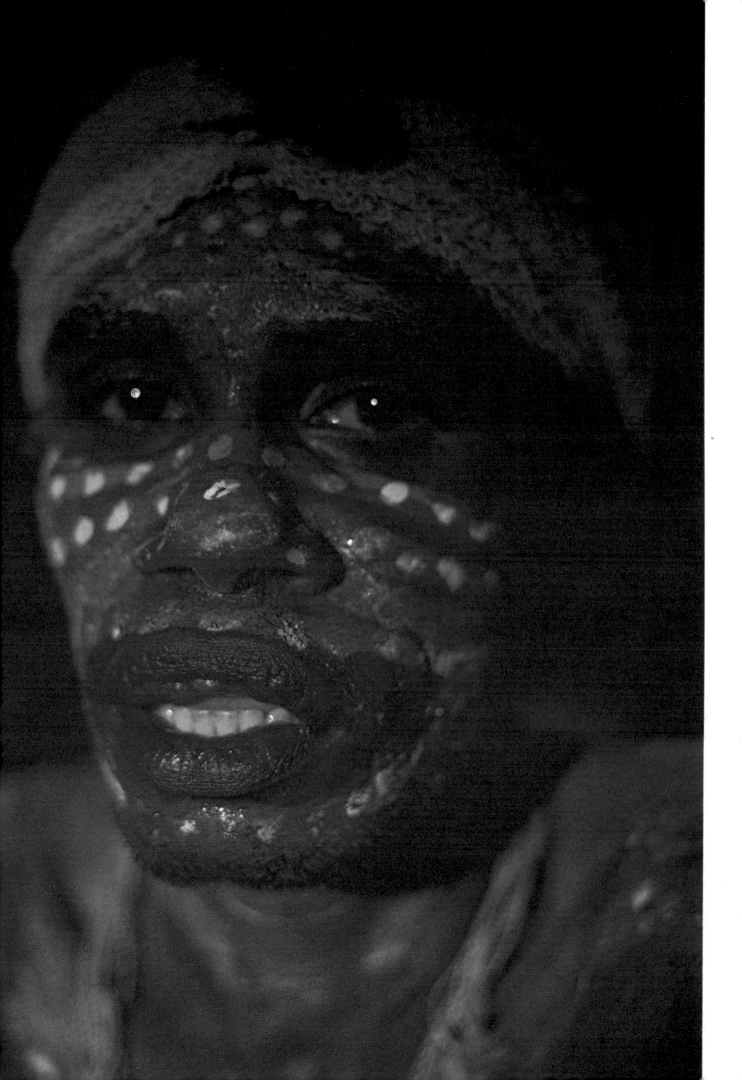

The Sacred Rocks on Elcho Island, like most unusual geological formations, have deep significance for the Aborigines. Here there are no taboos, for they move around the area quite freely. Crabs are plentiful and the fishing is good.

The ranggas of Elcho Island are sacred objects of exceptional significance; they symbolize the Aborigines' endeavour to adjust old traditions to new realities.

A fully initiated man on Elcho Island. These heavy incisions are made during manhood ceremonies; one so marked has great sexual attraction for women and the respect and admiration of men.

The decorative posts of Elcho Island often feature a carved face at the top which reflects Macassan influence.

the dreamtime, and may well be part of it; the legendary landing-places of the ancestral beings perhaps record recurrent migration waves untold centuries ago. The Macassan traders themselves, from the islands now known as Indonesia, came in relatively modern times, probably from about the sixteenth century. They came in spring, with the northwest monsoons, stayed for six months or more, seeking trepang (beche-de-mer) and pearl shell, then departed with the southeast winds of winter. They built their stilt houses, introduced the Aborigines to the dugout canoe and long Macassan pipe, and left their imprint on religious ritual, particularly burial ceremonies, symbol of farewell, which in many cases feature stylised ship's masts as raised by the Macassans before unfurling sails and returning to their homeland. This Macassan contact was by far the most significant so far as the Aborigines were concerned, though their songs also tell of the Badus in the northeast (Torres Strait Islanders) who were credited with sending the northeast winds which followed the wet season, and the coconuts and occasional "spirit" canoes which were tossed on their shores by the waves of those winds. They regarded the Badus as people not unlike themselves, and their legends tell that the islands there were the resting place of their dead, and the flotsam gifts sent by them to the living. The first European contact was by Dutch from Java in the seventeenth century. *Arnhem* was in the area in 1623, and left her name on the land. In 1636 another Dutch navigator, on *Wesel,* charted the coastline from the Wessel Group to Crocker Island. Abel Tasman sailed along the coast of Melville Island in 1644, though he mistook it for part of the mainland. Then Dutch interest slackened, for their mariners had failed to find hoped-for avenues for wealth and trade.

Children of Elcho play in a freshwater stream, watched by their teacher.

Pandanus on the beach at Elcho frame fishing boats in the bay.

The rocks of Elcho show a startling range of colours; these sombre black boulders contrast sharply with the bright pink and white and yellow of the Sacred Rocks pictured on the previous page.

Elcho Island woman weaving a mat. The women of the northern islands, always weavers of wild grasses into dilly bags, take easily to this mission-taught trade.

British exploration commenced in the early nineteenth century – Grant on *Lady Nelson*, Flinders on *Investigator* – and in 1818 Phillip Parker King surveyed much of the coastline and islands. The first attempt at settlement came a few years later – at Fort Dundas on Melville Island. It failed after five years, and today no signs remain, other than the herds of wild buffaloes, descendants of those brought from Timor in 1825.

The complex social organisation of the Aborigines is based broadly on two groups (moieties) each springing from one or more of the creative beings of Aboriginal mythology. These are the source of all fertility in the land. From them alone comes power and authority. They are the basis of the kinship system which defines behaviour and obligations. They order the rules of marriage, and set the pattern of music, art and dancing. The moieties that flow from them are further inter-woven in ways too complex to record here; suffice to say they are two halves of a whole. In every aspect of Aboriginal life they entwine with all their colourful strands, each moiety has its heritage of myths and rites, and both co-operate for ceremonies on the sacred nara grounds. Significant in the secret art of the moieties are the rangga, intricately carved poles of great beauty, sacred objects which, according to legend, have been given to them by their creative deities. These rangga are the visual proof that the moieties are following their myth-cycles, and their power is dependent upon them remaining hidden. They are seldom viewed by the uninitiated, never by women. An exception of extraordinary interest is the public display of rangga on Elcho Island. Professor R. M. Berndt describes this as an "adjustment" movement and records that it followed visits by a group of anthropologists, during which photographs were taken of sacred ceremonies and rangga. This in itself was disturbing, though apparently permitted by the elders. However, a film featuring the rangga was inadvertently shown to an

unrestricted audience at the Elcho Island mission church; not just the white outsiders, but the women and uninitiated of the tribe had viewed them and, according to tradition, they therefore lost all power. The elders of the day were Badangga, Buramara and Willy Wolili. All were closely associated with the Elcho Island mission, but still retained strong ties with their indigenous religion. They were caught between two worlds, and sometimes got the worst of both (it is reported that when a willy willy, twisting in from the sea, destroyed Buramara's hut, he was told on the one hand it was a *wonggar* from the dreamtime, punishing him because he had not fulfilled his ritual obligations, and on the other that God had sent it because he was backsliding). These leaders had long pondered the need to adjust traditional and introduced ways.

The changes from outside had brought benefits, but they could not be allowed to overwhelm the traditional society and culture. An answer was found in the incident of the exposed rangga, an answer which also restored to those sacred objects the power they had lost. Rangga would be created which characterised the outsiders, and the rangga of both cultures would stand side by side for all to view, a source of authority to the tribal elders and the white missionaries: "Mr. Shepherdson, he brought us new ways, he taught us everything. He put up buildings, planted gardens. Badangga is our leader. The missionaries call him that. With this memorial we make him a big leader, and all these rangga help him. Only the rangga are supreme. We want a leader for all the people, and bringing up the rangga gives him honour. So now he can look after things. Now we have to listen to Badangga, to Willy and to Mr. Shepherdson. They are supported by rangga."

70

The Sea Fox, stranded on the beach of Elcho Island by the great tides of the Arafura Sea, 1959. On board was Hollywood actor-magician John Calvert and also a chimpanzee, animal star of the Tarzan series. The incident had a tremendous impact on this isolated group of Aborigines; they had never seen a monkey before, and they were astounded by a man who could make things disappear before their eyes. This is the stuff of legends; a people of incredible memory, whose tales traditionally pass by word of mouth, they still speak of the "monkey ship" and the god-like creatures on it.

Djingalou, in his favourite billabong on Wessel Island. On the day this picture was taken a huge saltwater crocodile crawled out of the lagoon and half a mile across the sand to the sea, but this didn't worry Djingalou at all. Magpie geese feed by the thousand on these lagoons, seeking rikki nuts on water reeds; Aborigines hunt them for food.

St Andrew's Cross spider, Argiope aethera, on cashew nut tree, Elcho Island.

Ipomoea brasiliensis, the goats-foot morning glory, is a common beach flower on the northwest shore of Wessel Island. Below: Tiny green tree ants, incredibly strong, shape and bend huge leaves.

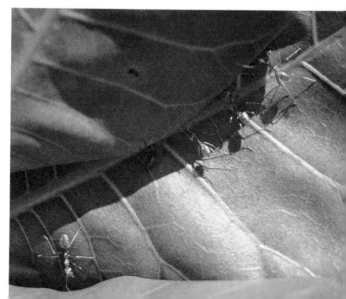

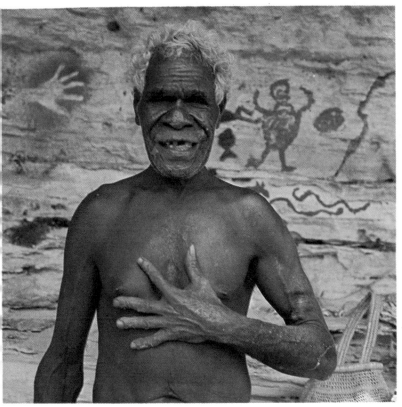

Wandamu, great artist of Elcho Island, gifted singer, dancer and song-reader. He paints sitting on the beach, and all his pictures tell a story.

String games, as played by the women of Elcho Island; these "cat's cradles" represent everyday actions and objects.

Djingalou, mouth covered with ochre, blows hand stencils in a cave on Wessel Island. An elder of that island, he has, like his fellows, left for the greener mission-pastures of nearby Elcho; Wessel today knows no permanent residents, only the periodic pilgrimages of expatriate Aborigines. In this cave Djingalou renews the legends of his ancestors, records the history of the present — in the group of drawings shown here he has depicted the fabulous monkey of the Sea Fox.

Both men and women smoke long Macassan pipes; Wandamu lights one.

Badangga made the white man's rangga, which features a cross. Explaining its significance, he said: "I believe in both ways – ours and the Christian. If we had taken both ways and thought of them separately we would have become confused. So we have selected the good laws from both and put them together." Nearby is a pulpit, decorated with Aboriginal motifs and sacred objects, from which Badangga gave sermons, wearing Aboriginal ritual dress. In front is a nara ground on which traditional singing and dancing takes place. Around the enclosure are nara-boards which read (in translation):
And this is the law of peace, helpful for us all.
This law will show us the way to be happy.
The leader Badannga has the memory of the old way –
Now we have changed our minds and worship God.
We will all come together as friends in one group.
We will follow that law, that way, that language.
The Aborigines placed tremendous importance on this memorial. To their mind they were offering the white man something tangible, their sacred rangga, their most precious possession. They expected reciprocity, European "rangga" in the form of schools and libraries. The movement was more than an endeavour to blend religions; it was an attempt to preserve the identity and self-assurance of the eastern Arnhem Landers, and at the same time to bridge the gap between old and new, to bring the advantages of the new culture to the Aborigines and enable them to play a more important role in the changed society. Invariably its emphasis is shifting from the sacred to the secular. The Aborigines not only desire to possess material goods of European origin, they also want the opportunity to achieve economic independence. Meetings of the council associated

Bathurst Islanders fish from a dugout canoe. Bathurst Island is an Aboriginal reserve; it lies, with neighbouring, much larger Melville Island, off the extreme western tip of Arnhem Land.

Saltwater crocodile, Crocodylus porosus; immense specimens occur in freshwater lagoons on the islands of Arnhem Land.

Man of Bathurst Island painting a mourning post. These posts carved from tree trunks feature in the spectacular burial rites of the Tiwi people (Melville and Bathurst Islanders). Up to fifteen feet high and painted with a variety of complex and colourful designs, they are not erected at the time of death but during mourning ceremonies commencing several months later and extending over a period. Three or four are put up in the initial ceremony, and perhaps a dozen or more added at intervals. These protracted burial rites emphasise the significance of death and the length of time the living require to adjust themselves to the shock received.

Bathurst Island Aborigine, with hair and beard worn in traditional style. The people of Arnhem Land and its adjacent islands show the Macassan influence.

Aborigines like to make their homes on the beach, as this family has at Elcho Island (the monkey ship, Sea Fox, can be seen in the background).

Apsley Strait, a channel fifty miles long and a mile wide, separates Bathurst and Melville Islands. It is affected by a very strong rip tide.

Djingalou collects turtle eggs on Wessel Island. He follows tracks to a likely spot, then probes the sand with a sharp stick, as the female turtle often lays false trails. If blood or yolk shows on the end of the stick, he starts digging.

Wildflowers of Wessel Island: A boy sucks honey from sugarbag grevillea, Grevillea pteridfolia, a native of the monsoon country of the tropical north. Gomphrena canescens, has rosy pink to purple flowers crowded into button-like heads; it rarely grows more than a foot high, and foliage is covered with long soft hairs. Yellow-flowered Dillenia alata, a native of Malaya and adjacent islands now naturalised on the islands of Arnhem Land, is a papery-barked tree which grows to sixty feet in height. Swamp grass on the sandy northwest shore is tall enough to hide a man.

with the movement are more and more engrossed with industrial relations with the white man, with questions of employment, attempts to regulate wages, and payments for work done or objects sold. Christianity and the traditional Aboriginal religion are hardly mentioned; indeed, the Aborigines find little difficulty in adjusting these. When Badangga died a few years ago, he was, as Church elder, given a Christian burial. This was followed by traditional Aboriginal mortuary rites extending over several months. Djingalou and Wandamu, pictured on these pages, are Christians, but, like most of the older men, they have, though married, their "promises" of younger women. These girls, despite mission training, invariably accept. The younger generation however tends to look more towards the mission and the Administration than to their own heritage, and the old tribal way of life is being inexorably broken down as the traditional small groups congregate in thousands around the focal point of mission, money, jobs and material advantages. (In this section Arnhem Land is regarded as being the roughly rhomboidal area at the top end of the Northern Territory, and its islands as extending from Bathurst and Melville in the west to the Wessels in the east – that long pointer to New Guinea which, though seldom more than a couple of miles across, varies dramatically in the seascape on either side. The northwest shore is sheltered and sandy; on the southeast are rocky shelves and cliffs up to a hundred feet high, crumbling into the sea in the face of weather far more severe. This group is a geographic crossroads, for the small marine animals of the western side are predominantly Australian, while those of the east show a strong New Guinean element.)

Rock painting by Djingalou (Wessel Island) demonstrates the Aborigines' close attention to detail and accuracy in recording the essentials of a subject. Art is the medium through which they record the news of the day and the various peoples who visit their islands. From the excellent detail of sails and ropes it is clear that this is a ketch-rigged vessel; it takes its place beside the Macassan praus of past ages, and bears the same strange x-ray patterns, indicating details of the interior.

These caves on the rocky southeast shore of Wessel Island contain extensive galleries of Aboriginal art.

ISLANDS OF ARNHEM LAND

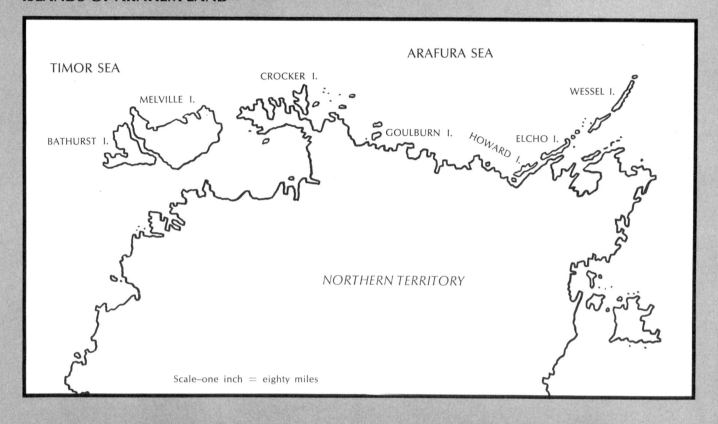

ARAFURA SEA

TIMOR SEA

CROCKER I.

MELVILLE I.

WESSEL I.

BATHURST I.

GOULBURN I.

HOWARD I.

ELCHO I.

NORTHERN TERRITORY

Scale—one inch = eighty miles

Dugong hunters depart from Mornington Island, perhaps to stay at sea for two or three days for they seldom return until they have caught one. Dugongs are mammals, and Aborigines listen for the sound of breathing, which they can hear from a considerable distance, or watch for bubbles on the surface. Dugongs and turtles have always been a main source of meat for the island tribes; today both animals are protected from all except Aborigines hunting them for food.

Aboriginal cave paintings at Groote Eylandt, Gulf of Carpentaria.

Mornington Islander in the typical stance of the Aborigine — relaxing on one leg. They will stand like this for hours — talking, watching, musing — and when seated will also fold their legs into incredible angles.

The Gulf of Carpentaria, that deep indentation on the northern coast of Australia, four hundred odd miles wide and penetrating the land for about the same distance, is virtually a rectangular sea bounded on three sides by almost straight coastlines. On the east is Cape York Peninsula, a continuation of the mountainous backbone of the Great Dividing Range of eastern Australia; on the west is the ancient rocky bastion of Arnhem Land. The southern shoreline is low and marshy, and was once the gateway to the great inland sea of Cretaceous times. The islands of the gulf lie along the western and southwestern shore: Groote Eylandt ("Great Island"), the largest – sighted and named by Tasman – and the nearby islands of Chasm, Bickerton and Woodah; then, sliding down the southwest coastline to Cape York Peninsula, the group named by Flinders for Sir Edward Pellew ("distinguished officer of the British Navy"), and the Wellesley Group – tucked in the protective armpit of the Peninsula itself.

These are also island outposts of the first Australians, but on Groote Eylandt, where development of manganese resources has brought the twentieth century in with a bang, the islanders face a situation similar to that of eighteenth-century Britain's industrial revolution, speeded up a thousandfold. This can only result in the complete disintegration of their traditional way of life, and it remains to be seen whether the twentieth century can replace it with something worthwhile.

Groote Eylandt people have had a long and varied association with other cultures. Macassan traders centuries ago looked on Australia's north coast as their own. They called it "Marege"; they explored it, pioneered it, and established trading bases. Against this background the casual and isolated early European visits passed virtually unnoticed until the mid-nineteenth century, when developing European enterprise led to open conflict with the Macassans. Customs depots were set up and efforts were made to extract duty from them. The long-standing partnership relationship with the Aborigines was disrupted; the pattern changed to adventurism, and the nineteenth-century Macassan trader attempted to evade the customs of both cultures. Friction developed, "Macassan massacres" occurred in which both Aborigines and Indonesians were killed, and in 1907 Macassan trading was banned. So ended an era; the Aborigines were then faced with the need to adjust to white adventurers and Japanese fishermen. These, unlike the Macassans, made no "partnership" arrangements. They did not employ Aborigines in their enterprises, nor desire trade with them (except in women). They simply took the sea harvest – and the women – which the Aborigines regarded as their own, and further massacres followed. This led to the creation, in the nineteen-thirties, of the Arnhem Land Reserve, a supposedly inviolable area where the Aborigines would be protected from outside influences other than that of the missions.

Groote Eylandt · Chasm Island · Sir Edward Pellew Group

Wellesley Group · Mornington Island · Bentinck Island

ISLANDS IN THE GULF OF CARPENTARIA

Groote Eylandt, an Aboriginal Reserve, is also a major centre of manganese production. Ore is carried in great vehicles over red dust roads a hundred yards wide, from the mines to long wharves which run far out into the sea, enabling vessels to be loaded at all times despite the high tide range.

Aborigines in many cases still pursue their old ways, for the present at least. Here one sucks sugarbag (wild bees' honey).

Wildflowers of Groote Eylandt, blooming in November. This is Cryptostegia grandiflora, native to Madagascar, now naturalized on the island.

However, World War II took Groote Eylandt to the front line of a twentieth-century war. An air force base was established, and this had the rather unexpected results of restoring the Aborigines' dwindling self-esteem and uniting not only the scattered tribal groups but also the semi-detribalised Aborigines congregated around the isolated missions. In some ways it was as if the old days of the early Macassans had come round again: once more they were partners in a joint enterprise, their labour was needed and had a value. They also came into contact for the first time with a new sort of white Australian – people who were neither missionaries (sometimes enlightened, sometimes paternalistic) nor adventurers (sometimes violent and ruthless, sometimes men of outstanding courage and initiative). They met a cross-section of ordinary blokes, and on the whole the meeting was a happy one. But this was a passing phase, which ended with the war. The manganese deposits which caught the eye of the entrepreneurs and led to the great industrial revolution of the sixties were known to the first Australians for centuries. They were the basis of their art: on Groote Eylandt the style of bark paintings generally consists of single or grouped figures on a plain manganese background (on Mornington Island the reverse is the case – black figures are against a white background). The ochres of Aboriginal art were the subject of widespread trade and exchange, so that each group had a full range, though each emphasised their own individual assets. Traded ochres, however, were always highly valued, and the various shades, traded from different localities, were named and carefully distinguished. Where their wet-season shelters were caves, rock paintings predominate. On the islands bark wet-shelters are the tradition, and in these areas bark paintings have reached a high stage of development. (Groote Eylandt has both, and Chasm Island is the enigma: a small, rocky outpost which could support only a limited population, but which nevertheless has a fantastic number of paintings in its numerous caves.) Aborigines use various natural fixatives for the pigments on their bark paintings – sap of tree orchids, wax and honey of wild bees, and yolks from the eggs of marine turtles. Brushes are made from chewed bark, orchid tubers, human hair or feathers. The bark itself is stripped from stringybark eucalypts; the selected piece is placed on a blazing fire for a few minutes, then the rough outer bark is removed and the pliable inner bark flattened. Aborigines sing a lot; often the words are meaningless, but it is also common practice for one to sing to another if he wishes to say something without attracting too much attention, particularly if he is criticising someone else. In the same way, all communications with superhuman beings are chanted or crooned, so that evil spirits will not notice. Dancing is also very much a part of Aboriginal life, and the corroboree is an important medium of expression practised by all – men, women and children. Dr Basedow, anthropologist and one-time Protector of Aborigines, says of the Aborigine: "By his dancing he impersonates both friend and enemy; he copies the hopping of the

In the isolation of the islands, Aborigines still follow the traditional way of life in many respects — hunting, food-gathering, singing and dancing as their ancestors have for countless years.

Very often music and art go together, in a casual, impromptu way; both are very much part of Aboriginal life, a medium of expression developed to a high level by a people who had no written language. The group shown here are relaxing on the beach at Groote Eylandt — some playing the didgeridoo, others painting on bark.

Corroboree headdress of a Mornington Islander; many hours or even days may be spent in preparation for these events.

Captive turtle is a plaything for these children of Mornington Island. When needed for food it will be slaughtered.

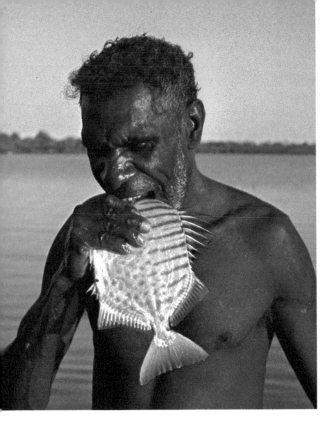

marsupial, or the wriggling of a serpent, or the strutting of an emu, and he emulates the legendary practices and sacred ceremonies of his forefathers. In his dances lives the valour of his warriors, and dies the evil image of his foes. Through his dances he endeavours to commune with the spirits of his dead, he hears the voices of his mythical demigods, and he beseeches his deities to protect his person and bless his haunts with an abundance of game." Mornington Island, about forty miles long and ten miles or so wide, is the largest of the Wellesley Group in the southern corner of the Gulf of Carpentaria. It is a happy island, one of the few remaining pockets of traditional Aboriginal happiness on this continent. There is no mining on Mornington, no threat of a wood chip industry as at Elcho, no violation of the land to which the Aborigine is bound by deep spiritual ties. The main industry is cattle grazing, which in no way runs counter to the Aboriginal ethos, and for the rest the islanders live by fishing and food-gathering, with some trade in artefacts. There is an excellent mission, under enlightened leadership; the Aborigines have been encouraged to retain their own culture, they are not detribalised, and the general atmosphere of the community is one of co-operation and mutual respect. There is, however, a notable exception. In addition to the indigenous Mornington Islanders – the Lardil people – there are two other groups of Aborigines on the island: mainland people from nearby Cape York Peninsula, and the Kaiadilt people – Bentinck Islanders and their progeny. Bentinck Island, second largest in the Wellesley group, was evacuated in 1948 following a severe drought, which threatened the tribe with extinction. These people, who differ remarkably from the Mornington Islanders in language and even blood groupings, are still, after so many years, suffering the effects of dislocation from their homeland. Many are emotionally disturbed, underlining the Aborigine's spiritual dependence on his tribal territory.

One quick bite, and the fish is dead!
This is the Aborigines' way of killing
fish, and they can dispose of a netful
with incredible speed.

A captured turtle is killed on the beach
at Mornington Island; all watch,
including the children who may earlier
have had it for temporary playmate.
They watch with detachment; like
their parents, they are essentially practical.
Everything is used but not abused;
the animal must die to provide food.

Netting for fish and mudcrabs
around the mangrove- lined shores,
Mornington Island.

Chasm Island owes its name to the huge
caves and chasms that dissect its cliffs,
some cutting right through from one side
to the other. These caves contain many
outstanding examples of Aboriginal art.

A mob of horses swimming the
shark-infested waters between Mornington
and Denham Islands — a distance of one
and a half miles. This was one of the most
terrifying sights the author has ever
witnessed. It occurred during the dry
season and the horses, already weakened
by lack of food, faced a double peril
from sharks and exhaustion. They were
led by Aboriginal stockmen, seeking
better feeding grounds for them.

End game of the turtle; Aboriginal
mother gives the shell to her children
for a play-boat. This is the Aboriginal
attitude, to make use of all things that
come his way; nothing is ever wasted.

ISLANDS IN THE GULF OF CARPENTARIA

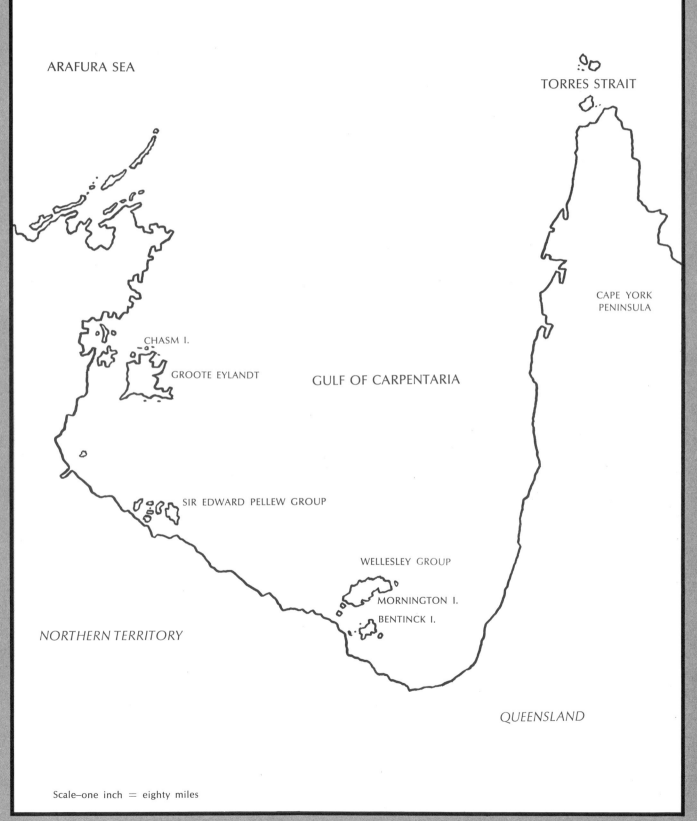

ARAFURA SEA

TORRES STRAIT

CAPE YORK
PENINSULA

CHASM I.

GROOTE EYLANDT

GULF OF CARPENTARIA

SIR EDWARD PELLEW GROUP

WELLESLEY GROUP

MORNINGTON I.

BENTINCK I.

NORTHERN TERRITORY

QUEENSLAND

Scale—one inch = eighty miles

The islands of Torres Strait; Thursday Island is in the foreground. The origin of the European "calendar" names of some Torres Strait Islands is obscure: Bligh, in his epic journey in the Bounty's longboat from Tahiti to Timor, named Sunday and Wednesday; Cook is said to have named Thursday but this name does not appear on charts before 1850.

Japanese craftsman culturing pearls on Friday Island, and (opposite page) the finished product. Cultured pearls thrive in Australian waters; they grow more quickly than in the seas around Japan where the technique was first perfected, and several farms have been established in the Torres Strait Islands.

Thursday Island   ·   Friday Island   ·   Hammond Island

Horne Island   ·   Possession Island   ·   Albany Island

Adolphus Island   ·   Banks Island

Prince of Wales Island

ISLANDS OF TORRES STRAIT

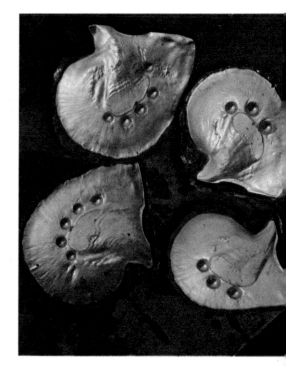

Torres Strait, the narrow, shallow seaway which separates Australia from New Guinea, is dotted with numerous islands ranging in size from Prince of Wales Island, some seventy square miles in area, to coral cays, reefs and sandbanks barely above sea level. One can sail for days in Torres Strait and never once lose sight of land. In past geological ages the strait was dry, and formed the land link to New Guinea. The high western islands – Prince of Wales, Horne, Tuesday, Wednesday, Thursday and Friday – are simply the northern termination of the Great Dividing Range of eastern Australia, drowned by rising sea levels. They are rocky, hilly islands, covered with sparse vegetation. Then come the coral cays, continuation of Australia's Great Barrier Reef, and further eastward, the volcanic islands of the Murray Group, supporting rich tropical vegetation.

The original Torres Strait Islanders physically resembled the Papuans rather than the Australian Aborigines, but there was a curious language division between the western and eastern islanders – the western languages being related to those of mainland Australia and the eastern to New Guinea – and, on the whole, the western and eastern peoples appear to have kept fairly strictly to their respective areas. Today's Torres Straitsmen are a cosmopolitan population, descendants of many races, original inhabitants and others lured or lumbered to the islands by discovery of gold and the rich pearling days that followed: Europeans, Japanese, Malays and Indonesians, Pacific Islanders, indentured New Guineans and Aborigines from the Australian mainland. Thursday Island is today the most important, the administrative centre for the whole area. Though small, rocky and barren – not considered suitable for habitation by the original peoples of these parts – it is situated on the best passage through the treacherous Torres Straits, has the advantage of being sheltered by the five or six larger islands which surround it, and possesses the safest port and anchorage.

Spanish navigator Torres was the first European known to penetrate the strait which now bears his name. The discovery was an unwilling one; Torres intended sailing northward to the Solomons but was trapped by the prevailing southeast monsoon and forced to creep slowly and cautiously westward through the shoals and sandbanks along the south coast of New Guinea. In September, 1606, he reached and landed on the Isla de los Perros (Isle of Dogs) which is the Daru of today. Torres and his men landed also on several other islands – Banks (Moa) was probably the most southerly – and climbed to vantage points to survey their surroundings; what they saw pleased them not one whit. They found themselves hemmed in by shoals, extensive reefs and numerous islands – at one point they counted forty – and they were weeks wending their way through the islands of Torres Strait. In the same year, a few months earlier, Dutch navigator Jansz on *Duyfken* (first European known to land on the Australian mainland) approached the

area from the east, sailed up the western coastline of Cape York Peninsula, and noted the various islands and extensive coral reefs of Torres Strait. The same prevailing winds and tides which drove Torres through prevented him from entering it. Jansz was followed by other Dutchmen, also from the east – Carstenz, Tasman – but none passed through the strait again until Captain James Cook in 1770 entered it, like Torres, from the west. Cook sighted Thursday Island, named Booby and Prince of Wales, and landed on Possession, where he and his party "hoisted English Coulers" and "in the name of his Majesty King George the Third took possession of the whole Eastern Coast . . . by the name of New South Wales together with all the Bays Harbours Rivers and Islands . . ."

There was treachery and tragedy on the islands of Torres over the following century. The islanders had the habit of murdering shipwreck survivors – perhaps merely for economic reasons as food supplies were limited by the area of their islands. (They practised infanticide for this reason: "family planning" which consisted of ruthlessly restricting the number of children to two or three.) On the part of the Europeans, there was much aggression and more than ample reprisal, starting with Torres who records robbing native plantations and taking on board three women "for the service of the crew" and extending to 1877, five years after the annexation of the islands into the colony of Queensland. In that year the white crew of the *Sherwer*, seventeen in number, were slaughtered by the people of Muralug (Prince of Wales Island) and in reprisal the whole population was rounded up; men, women and children were destroyed, their bodies thrown into a waterhole. On the other hand, there were some instances of compassion. When the *Charles Eaton* was lost in Torres Strait in 1834, eight survivors – six men, two women and two children – reached one of the islands. The adults were killed, but the children were spared and reared by the islanders of Mer. When rescued two years later it is reported that these little boys wept for days at the enforced parting from their native friends. There is also the story of Barbara Thompson, the wild white woman of Possession Island, who was rescued after four years with the Muralug people. She had found more to fear from the strange white man who lived and reigned on Badu (Mulgrave Island). Bêches-de-mer, prized by Chinese for centuries as a delicacy and aphrodisiac and now under investigation by scientists who report a possibility that the strange, slug-like sea animals may be useful in control of cancer, were the basis of the first industry in Torres Strait, hundreds of years before the coming of white men, when Malays and Chinese made their seasonal visits to fish these waters. The islanders also valued pearlshell, which they used for ornament (though, curiously, they ignored the pearls). Japanese and Europeans entered both industries in the last century, and there is a large and colourful Japanese community on Thursday Island. The islanders, themselves excellent divers, developed their own fishing fleet, the boats of which are owned by the island community as a whole. In recent years cultured pearl farms have been established.

Torres Strait and the northern extremity of Cape York Peninsula.

Somerset and Albany Island. The Quetta was wrecked near here in 1890, with a loss of over one hundred and fifty lives. Joseph Conrad, who passed through Torres Strait in the barque Otago in 1887 (probably the last ship to do so under sail) reported that his first and last views of Torres were of wrecked ships.

ISLANDS OF TORRES STRAIT

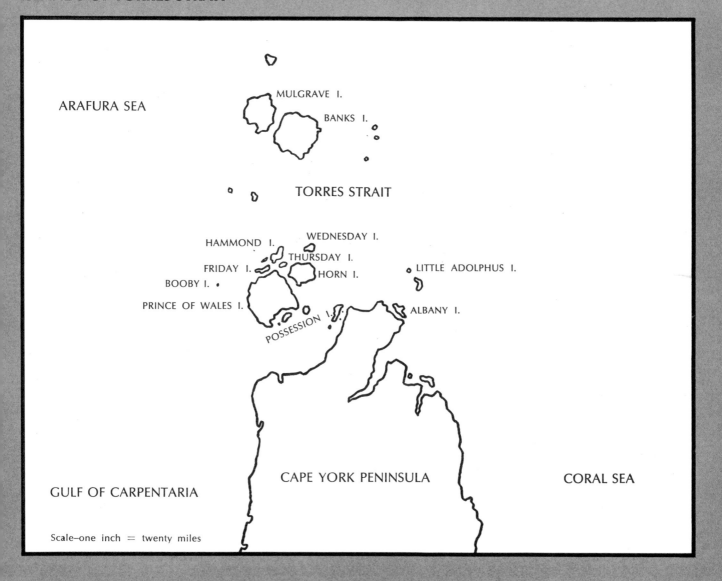

ARAFURA SEA

MULGRAVE I.

BANKS I.

TORRES STRAIT

WEDNESDAY I.

HAMMOND I.

THURSDAY I.

FRIDAY I.

HORN I.

LITTLE ADOLPHUS I.

BOOBY I.

PRINCE OF WALES I.

POSSESSION I.

ALBANY I.

CAPE YORK PENINSULA

CORAL SEA

GULF OF CARPENTARIA

Scale—one inch = twenty miles

CORAL SEA ISLANDS

Giant sea anemone, Physobrachia *species, is common on the Great Barrier Reef; its tentacles provide a haven for certain colourful small fish.*

Pisonia trees are the dominant and sometimes only arboreal growth on the coral cays. They form dense jungle-like forests of relatively tall trees. Boles are often massive and fantastically buttressed, but the tree is soft-wooded and limbs are treacherously brittle.

Islands of the Bunker Group. Fairfax is in the foreground, Lady Musgrave in the distance. These coral cays, among the most southerly of the Barrier Reef, lie just below the Tropic of Capricorn.

Australia's islands of the Coral Sea are scattered along the coast of Queensland. There are the low islands, coral cays of the Barrier Reef, and the high or "continental" islands, coral-fringed peaks of a former coastal range. Further south is Fraser Island, massive verdant sand dune isolated from the mainland by rising seas of the last ice age. Collectively they comprise one of the wonders of the world, for Australia's Great Barrier Reef is the mightiest coral structure in existence.

It encompasses an area of over eighty thousand square miles and extends for more than twelve hundred miles – from just south of the Tropic of Capricorn almost to New Guinea. In the north the coral banks, laced with an intricate labyrinth of twisting channels, are up to fifty miles across. Seaward the margin is marked by a mighty line of thundering breakers, where the Great Barrier itself faces the fiercest surf in the world, whipped by winds of the wide Pacific. This rampart rises from the margin of the continental shelf, from depths greater than a thousand fathoms. It extends in an almost unbroken chain of ribbon-like reefs from Torres Strait to Trinity Opening, near Cairns. South of this point it is less defined, diverging from the coastline and gradually becoming a scattered collection of isolated reeferies, almost two hundred miles out to sea.

Rising from the shallower parts of the sheltered lagoon that lies between this rampart and the mainland are a myriad reefs and coral cays, and the clustered high islands, skirting the coast. These, rather than the awesome outriders, comprise the "Great Barrier Reef" for most Australians. The reef teems with life, in a bewildering variety of colour, form and size. It is itself a living thing, built by tiny animals of the lowly Coelentrata group, relatives of the jellyfish and sea anemone who have acquired the protective ability to secrete lime. These colourful fleshy polyps build around and within their tissues a hard calcareous skeleton, and on their stony remains, often of intricate and delicate design, the living reef builds.

Reefs are formed from the interlocked and encrusted skeletons of corals, coralline algae and molluscs. They support a complex community of reef-dwelling plants and animals, and exist in uneasy equilibrium between the forces of construction and destruction, a constantly repeated cycle of building up and tearing down. The forces which destroy and tear down the reef are often but another facet of those which build it. Cementing algae sometimes smother living coral. Waves which physically consolidate debris around the coral framework may batter and break the structure formed, dislodging great blocks and reducing them to rubble. No less important though less obvious is the relentless activity of the reef-dwelling marine life itself. Algae, worms, molluscs, echinoderms, are constantly at work, boring into the consolidated coral, dissolving it, breaking it down into a fine sand which is in turn re-located by wind and wave to buttress other reefs and build the coral cays. Hundreds of different coral species contribute to the building of the reefs, but in the main they fall into two categories – the delicate branching staghorns and the rounded boulder-like brain and star corals. Most combine to form a colony, but some are solitary in habit, such as the mushroom coral (*Fungia* species) a solitary polyp which grows to the size of a dinner plate. All true reef-building corals have hard, white skeletons, the colour of the living colonies is confined to the fleshy polyps.

Green Island, near Cairns, one of the closest and most accessible of the true coral cays. The magnificent coral reefs which surround it are threatened by a plague of crown-of-thorns starfish, perhaps triggered by interference in the ecology caused by pesticides and fertilizers washed from the nearby mainland, or depletion by shell gatherers of tritons, the natural predator.

Blue pullers, Chromis caeruleus, dart in and out of the coral with incredible swiftness.

Crowded reef flat, Michaelmas Cay.

In recent years destruction of coral by the crown-of-thorns starfish has caused considerable concern. A few years ago this starfish was very rare and seldom seen; it had not been studied to any extent and very little was known about it. Under the present plague conditions it feeds on coral polyps, particularly those of the reef-building hard corals, battalions moving remorselessly over the coral colonies at the rate of about a foot a minute, each starfish digesting daily an area of living polyps twice its own size. In some localities it has devastated vast areas of living reef. Acres of great branching staghorns, formerly a kaleidoscope of vivid purple, orange, green and blue, stand ashen-grey and lifeless like mighty forests ravaged by bushfires. Here and there huge clumps have collapsed, fallen giants tumbled on the sea floor, shattered branches scattered on the sand. Gone are the colourful coral fish and other gay denizens of the complex reef community. Gone, too, are the crown-of-thorns starfish. Only the great clams remain, and the desolate dead coral, cloaked in a sombre winding-sheet of slowly spreading algae. (Dr. J. H. Barnes of Queensland has advanced the theory that this extensive algal growth on dead coral could be the origin of ciguatera-type neurotoxins now present in the flesh of some herbivorous fish – a theory of special interest to the authors because the eating of ciguatera-bearing fish causes an extremely painful and potentially fatal illness in man – as Douglass Baglin well knows, having suffered from it on a recent voyage among the islands of the South Pacific; he owes his life to the United States Apollo Spacecraft air-sea recovery team, who staged a dramatic rescue from Malden, in the Line Islands, and flew him sixteen hundred miles to hospital in Honolulu. However, there is no evidence as yet of ciguatera poisoning in Australian waters.)

What caused the crown-of-thorns plague? What led to the population explosion that triggered this starfish to destroy its own environment? Theories are many, facts are few. Very little is known of

Acanthaster planci except under the plague conditions which have thrust it latterly into the limelight of research. Scientists frankly declare that knowledge is meagre about the biology of reef fauna and the physical environment in which they live; that the cause of the initial population build-up of the crown-of-thorns is just not known. One widely canvassed possible cause is the removal by tourists and shell-collectors of the giant triton, a large mollusc-predator of adult starfish. But since this shellfish can dispose of only one fullgrown starfish per week per head, and since the frantic efforts of skin-divers employed by tourist resorts – resulting in a record catch of nearly four hundred in a single day – have failed to halt the advancing horde to any significant extent, it is obvious that, whether or not they are the cause, tritons cannot be the cure of this disorder. They cannot regenerate the reefs destroyed, and, if placed in sufficient numbers on threatened reefs, could well tip the imbalance in favour of faster devastation. Other theories revolve around the "chicken and egg" premise: which came first? It has been argued that the crown-of-thorns assumes plague proportions initially on areas where the reef is dying – in much the same way that worms and fleas infest a sick animal. It is also held that the plague arose as a result of some deficiency of normal predators of the larval stage – and these include the coral polyp itself. (Since a female starfish can produce up to twenty-four million eggs a breeding season, and since the adult is armed with a thicket of thorny spines which defy most predators, control in the juvenile stages would appear to be crucial. Whichever came first, it is obvious that the crown-of-thorns population build-up is a vicious circle: as more and more coral is destroyed, more and more larval starfish survive to reach maturity.) Theories on the degeneration of areas of coral range from the effects of pesticides, fertilizers and other pollutants washed from the nearby mainland to changes in the ecology due to an unexplained rise in overall sea temperatures in recent years – possibly caused by underwater explosions of atomic devices. On the other hand, some hold that the present situation is a cyclic phenomenon which has occurred before and will right itself in time. We just don't know. Further research is essential and imperative. Amid the flurry of theories, two frightening facts have emerged: the starfish has reached plague proportions in other parts of the world's oceans, and there are reefs showing signs of degeneration in areas where the crown-of-thorns has not yet been reported.

We do however know the result of oil pollution on coral formations and other marine life and we **can** control the cause. One could wonder why some Australians see the necessity to increase the risks to the Reef in search of something that could well be redundant before existing known supplies are exhausted. Viewing the present and potential destruction of Australia's unique natural assets in the name of progress and prosperity, one is moved to echo the philosophy of Omar Khayyam:

*"I often wonder what the Vintners buy
One half so precious as the Goods they sell."*

Corals on Arlington Reef; soft green alcyonarian coral and Acropora species.

Deep sea red coral and flag-tail surgeon fish, Paracanthurus hepatus.

Reef clam, Tridacna maxima, noted for the seemingly endless variety of colour and pattern of its fleshy mantle.

The butterfly cod, Pterois volitans, moves through the water with the grace of a ballet dancer, trailing bright fans of greatly enlarged fins. A member of the dreaded scorpion fish family, it can afford to take its time; the decorative featherlike fin-spines are venom-tipped.

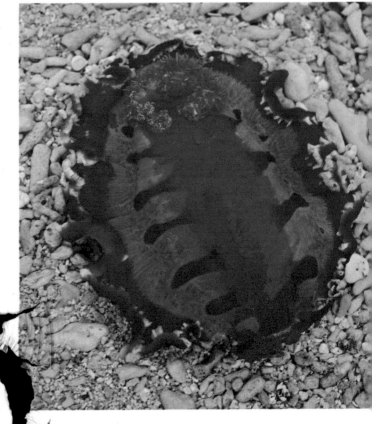

Red-mouth stromb, Strombus (Conomurex) luhuanus, *is common on the reef flats.*

Baby turtles, newly hatched by sun and sand, face a perilous journey to the sea, braving ghost crabs by night and silver gulls by day. Very few reach the water.

Sand-dwelling ghost crabs, Ocypoda ceratophtalma, *are rarely seen abroad in daylight, but emerge from their subterranean quarters after dusk, moving in battalions over the wet sand, stalked eyes protruding like periscopes over boulders and broken coral.*

Dancing lady, Hexabranchus imperialis, *a nudibranch, is one of the loveliest creatures of the reef. These are sea slugs, molluscs without shells; they move with sinuous grace, dancing and undulating over and around the coral.*

Harlequin tusk fish, Lienardella fasciatus, *and colourful sea-cucumber,* Cucumaria tricolor, *shown here feeding with characteristic ring of tentacles fully extended. This is a holothurian, relative of the drab beches-de-mer.*

Sea turtles, ancient reptiles who returned to the oceans during the dynasty of the dinosaurs, are still linked to the land they left so long ago. Each nesting season they must seek the sand and sun. From late spring to early autumn they come to the coral cays; they come at dusk, on the incoming tide, instinctively returning to the same beaches, sometimes travelling great distances from their normal feeding grounds. With many a laboured sigh the female heaves her ponderous bulk up the sloping sand, lurching forward with the aid of powerful flippers until she reaches her chosen spot, well above high tide level and usually beneath the protective canopy of casuarina or tournefortia trees. Here she sets about excavating her nest, scooping sand out with front flippers and shovelling it back with the hind ones. She may dig several depressions before finally depositing her clutch of fifty to two hundred round, leathery "ping-pong" eggs. All the time, tears stream down her cheeks, but this sad weeping is rather to keep the sand from her eyes, than self-pity or fretting over the possible fate of her hatchlings. When finished she replaces the sand and returns to the sea. The eggs are incubated by the heat of the sun, the period depending upon the temperature; once hatched, the baby turtles clamber out of the nest and make their perilous way to the sea, braving ghost crabs by night and silver gulls by day. Few survive the journey – ants scavenge the carapaces that litter the sand.

Iridescent beetles, Tectocoris
diophthalmus, *vary greatly in colour.
Pink native lasiandra,* Melastoma
denticulata, *nicker nuts,* Guilandina
bonduc, *and yellow* Thunbergia *species
are common on the islands.*

*Old weighing station on Lady Musgrave,
said to have been erected by Zane Grey.*

*Noddy terns nest on Pisonia trees; stilt
rooted pandanus grow on coral rubble.*

Hinchinbrook, largest of the high islands which skirt the coastline of northern Queensland. These islands are peaks of drowned mountains, relics of a bygone coastal range; they mirror the mountainous mainland, rising abruptly from the sea to spectacular craggy peaks. Hinchinbrook is a wild and rugged island, covered with dense tropical vegetation and deeply indented by mangrove-lined creeks. A national park, it is separated from the mainland by winding Hinchinbrook Channel, a long fault valley drowned in Tertiary times.

Horse-tail casuarina or coast she-oak, Casuarina equisetifolia var. incana, grows on almost pure sand, forming the vanguard of larger vegetation.

The crowded islands and narrow channels of the Whitsunday Passage make the area one of the scenic wonders of the world. These high islands support rich tropical vegetation and the fringing coral reefs as yet have not known the ravages of the crown-of-thorns starfish. Exploratory undersea drilling for oil is proposed at nearby Repulse Bay, on the mainland.

Vegetation on the high islands is similar to that of the nearby mainland. Eucalypts predominate; wattles and melaleucas are common. Dark-crowned hoop pines, hoary with grey-green lichen, grow on the boulder-strewn hillsides; rainforest trees, festooned with epiphytic orchids, ferns and vines, crowd the moist gullies. The flora of the coral cays is also derived from the mainland, borne thence by ocean currents, winds and wandering sea birds. Stilt-rooted pandanus grow in coral rubble by the sea's edge; the buoyant fruits are carried by the waves, as are those of the tournefortia, a low, widespreading shrub which crowds in thickets on the coral strands. Pisonia trees, the dominant growth on many islands, owe their wide dispersal to sea birds; seed vessels are covered with a sticky substance and mature when the legions of white-capped noddies nest among the branches. These adhere to feet and feathers and are carried far and wide when the birds depart. (Sometimes smaller or weaker ones become so covered with the seeds that they are trapped, and the pisonia is called the "bird-catching tree" for this reason.) The coast she-oak or horsetail casuarina has winged seeds, readily distributed by wind. It establishes itself on almost pure sand, fringing the beaches, bearing the brunt of high-velocity seasonal winds; graceful, drooping foliage curtains the sand, providing the filtered sunlight and shade sought by nesting turtles. In more sheltered places these trees may attain great age and size.

Coral islands of the Bunker Group. Hoskyn, Lady Musgrave, Fairfax — and opposite, a wave-washed exposed reef, an island in the making. These are the low islands of the inner platform reefs which lie between the mainland and the Great Barrier itself — elongated, leeward-pointing cays formed of consolidated sand and broken coral built up towards the lee end of the reefs by the action of wind and waves. Seldom more than a few feet above sea level, they are colonized by wind- and wave-borne vegetation, and range from tiny mounds of coral shingle sparsely clothed with stunted grass to islands several square miles in area, supporting dense forests of tall trees and appearing to be much higher than they actually are. They are nesting places for migratory birds and sea turtles, and in season support prolific life. The inner reefs on which they form are horseshoe-shaped, moulded by wind-whipped currents to lie with their longer axis parallel to the prevailing tradewinds; they encircle sheltered, deep lagoons and sometimes support a ring of cays — a pseudo-atoll.

Uprooted casuarina on the coral shingle, conquered by seasonal monsoon winds.

Coconut palms on Magnetic Island, near Townsville. Coconuts are common on both the high and low islands. Fruit, encased in a hard woody shell and protected by a thick fibrous husk, floats readily and is widely distributed. However, though germinating nuts are frequently seen amongst the flotsam cast up on the coral beaches, most of the palms now growing on the islands have been planted by man.

The New Endeavour, sailing through Whitsunday Passage, recaptures the wonder of Cook's voyage. On June 4th, 1770, he wrote: "Winds at SSE and SE, a gentle breeze and clear weather. In the PM steer'd thro the passage . . . formed by the Main on the West and by Islands on the East . . . everywhere a good anchorage; indeed the whole passage is one continued safe harbour, besides a number of small Bays and Coves on each side where Ships might lay as it were in a Bason . . . The land, both on the Main and the Islands, is Tolerably high and distinguished by Hills and Vallies which are diversified with Woods and Lawns that looked green and pleasant. This passage I have named Whitsunday's Passage, as it was discovered on the day the Church commemorates that Festival . . ."

Cook, in 1770, was the first European mariner to report on the waterways and islands of the Great Barrier Reef, though undoubtedly sailors from the north had for centuries explored the area, seeking the prized bêches-de-mer. Legend also has it that Spanish galleons lie wrecked on the Reef, and Spanish coins and cannon have been found on the islands. In 1789 Bligh passed that way on his epic journey by open boat from Tahiti to Timor after being cast adrift with eighteen of his crew following the mutiny of the *Bounty.* Two years later, in 1791, he was followed by HMS *Pandora,* with fourteen of the captured *Bounty* mutineers. These unfortunates were housed in a wooden crate built on the deck for that purpose which they styled, with grim humour, "Pandora's Box." James Morrison, petty officer, one of their number, described it as being eleven feet by eighteen, and the heat when it was calm "so intense that the sweat frequently ran to the scuppers and produced maggots in a short time . . . ," so it is doubtful if these early, unwilling tourists had much of an eye for the wonders of Australia's Coral Sea islands. Nor, apparently, did the ship's company; Edwards, *Pandora's* captain, described the area as a "huge unexplored chaos" – a prophetic term for *Pandora* was wrecked on the Reef in Torres Strait, and ninety survivors in four boats journeyed to Timor in the wake of Bligh. The difficulties that Bligh had faced were multiplied: Edwards had more boats, more people, and less water. He did however have a copy of Bligh's map, which was of greater use to him when he too was navigating small boats than when seeking a passage through the reef in *Pandora.* In the same year, a few months earlier, escaped convicts William and Mary Bryant, with their two small children, a three-year-old girl and a babe in arms, and accompanied by seven others, made the voyage up the coast and around Cape York to Timor. They travelled in "an open six oar Boat – having of provision on Bd one hundred wt of flower and one hundd st of Rice 14 lb of pork and aBout Eight galons of water . . ." according to the record of James Martin, one of the convicts who accompanied them. He describes the difficulties encountered: "I will Leave you to Consider what distress we muust be in the Woman and the two little Babies was in a bad Condition everything being so Wet that we Cou'd by no Means light a Fire we had nothing to Eat except a little raw rice at Night . . . " The perilous three thousand mile journey was made in sixty-nine days, without loss of life. On their arrival they posed as shipwreck survivors and were entertained by the Dutch – the British Government later footed the bill – until exposed by Edwards and the *Pandora* survivors. Bryant and the baby died soon after

Indian Head, Fraser Island — an isolated outcrop of rock on an island of sand.

Grave of Banfield ("The Beachcomber") on Dunk Island; the inscription reads: "If a man does not keep pace with his companions, perhaps it is because he hears the music of a different drummer. Let him step to the music he hears."

The Amos Tree, mighty casuarina on Musgrave. Below: turtles lay their eggs in the filtered sun and shade of these trees.

Islands of the Whitsunday Passage from 26,000 feet. These are the high or "continental" islands; all are hilly. Patterns of sea currents in the passage can be seen in this aerial view.

Prevailing winds have caused a blowout on denuded areas of Fraser Island, and sand dunes smother further vegetation. The island is itself a massive sand dune, seventy miles long. Luxuriant with rain forests and deep freshwater lakes, it is the largest island off the Queensland coast, a pendulous guardian of the Great Barrier Reef. Formed in an earlier age, when winds were fiercer and the coastline lay further east, it is slowly but surely being eroded by the sea, doomed from the time that melting ice-caps left it to the mercy of ocean currents.

Prevailing winds and ocean currents build a long sandspit on Fairfax Island.

being taken into custody; the little girl, Charlotte (named for the First Fleet vessel on which she was born), died on the way to England, as did three others. Captain Watkin Tench, who came to the colony on the *Charlotte* which brought the Bryants, and returned to England on the *Gorgon* which took Mary and the others back, wrote: "I confess that I never looked at these people without pity and astonishment. They had miscarried in an heroic struggle for liberty and after having combated every hazard and conquered every difficulty. The woman and one of the men had gone out to Botany Bay on the same ship which took me thither. They had both been distinguished for good behaviour." (The man was James Martin.) The Bryants were followed by Flinders, in 1802. He made extensive charts of the area – some of which are still in use today – and threaded his way through the Reef via the passage near Townsville which now bears his name. Ebor Bunker, pioneer whaler from America, surveyed and gave his name to the Bunker Group a few years later. These are some of the known stories of those who in the past ventured among Australia's archipelagos of the Coral Sea, but relics on the Reef indicate that many tales, perhaps equally dramatic, are unrecorded. There is on Lady Musgrave Island a mighty casuarina, discovered by Douglass Baglin on a recent trip to the area. On the massive trunk of this centuries-old tree is an inscription; calloused bark, inches thick, has crept back across the weathered blaze but the name "A. Amos" and the figures "7 9 5" can still be deciphered. 1795? or does it record the seventh day of the ninth month, some year in the eighteen-fifties? This is but one of many unexplained mysteries of the Reef.

Destroyers of the reefs and islands of the Coral Sea: Crown-of-thorns starfish, Acanthaster planci, and feral goats, left on the islands last century as a potential meat supply for shipwrecked sailors. One has eaten out large areas of coral, the other has denuded the cays.

Lady Elliott Island, most southerly of the coral cays, is now virtually treeless as a result of depredation by goats.

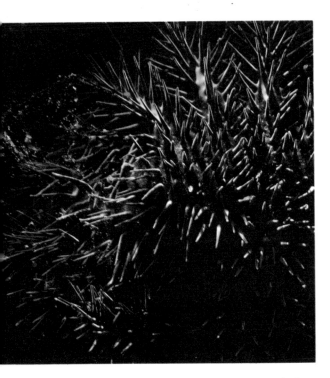

CORAL SEA ISLANDS

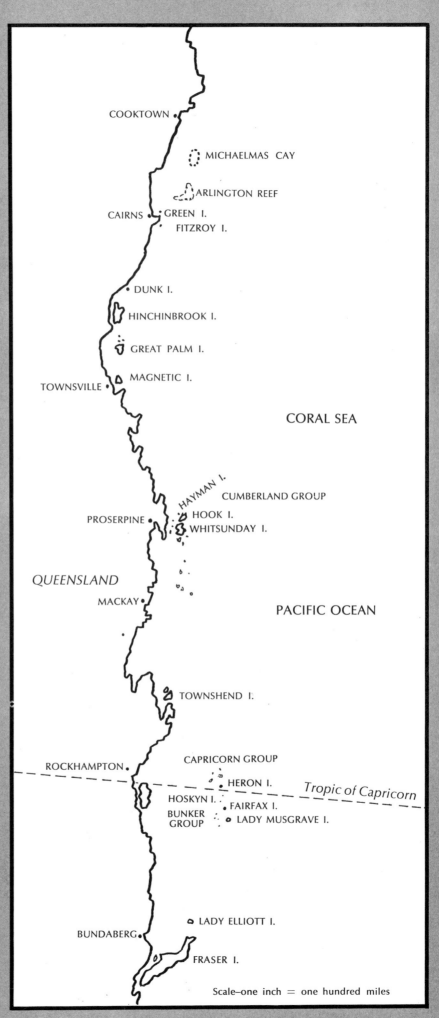

COOKTOWN

MICHAELMAS CAY

ARLINGTON REEF

CAIRNS • GREEN I.
FITZROY I.

• DUNK I.

HINCHINBROOK I.

GREAT PALM I.

MAGNETIC I.

TOWNSVILLE •

CORAL SEA

HAYMAN I.
CUMBERLAND GROUP
HOOK I.
PROSERPINE • WHITSUNDAY I.

QUEENSLAND

MACKAY • PACIFIC OCEAN

TOWNSHEND I.

CAPRICORN GROUP
ROCKHAMPTON •
HERON I. *Tropic of Capricorn*
HOSKYN I. •
• FAIRFAX I.
BUNKER • LADY MUSGRAVE I.
GROUP

LADY ELLIOTT I.

BUNDABERG •
FRASER I.

Scale—one inch = one hundred miles

ISLANDS OF THE TASMAN SEA

The crescent-moon of Lord Howe Island, isolated outpost in a thousand miles of ocean, lies where the Coral Sea meets the Tasman. Sheltered in the curve of the crescent is a shallow lagoon, guarded by a coral reef, the most southerly in the world – corals flourish there because a branch of the warm South Equatorial Current sweeps downward past the island, keeping the sea temperatures always above the minimum necessary for reef-coral growth. The island itself is less than seven miles long and never more than a mile wide, dominated by two massive, sheer-sided mountains of black basalt, Mounts Gower and Lidgbird, which form the southern half. These isolated peaks, warmed by tropic seas, are hit by chill winds blowing unchecked from Antarctica, so that clouds form constantly; tree-ferns and palms, hung with mosses and lichens, grow on the mist-shrouded plateaus, and the moist ground is carpeted with sphagnum. It is on these almost inaccessible mountain tops, and the hanging valley between them, that the rarer fauna of Lord Howe still survives. (A small colony of brown-headed petrels, Norfolk Island's "bird of Providence" which was exterminated within a decade by early settlers there, was recently discovered on Mount Gower.)

The northern part of the island is also composed of basaltic hills, the "younger volcanics" lower and less spectacular than the ancient peaks of the southern end; the two halves are linked by low-lying land formed from wind-blown sand and fragmented coral and sea-shells, consolidated into a coarse-grained sandy limestone. Each area has its own characteristic vegetation – on the lowlands, mighty banyans trail curtains of aerial roots in the central forests; *Howea* palms and buttressed *Pandanus* trees, endemic to the island and taller than those of the mainland, line the beaches. Clustered around the main island are a dozen or more tiny islets and rocks – the Admiralty Islets in the north, Rabbit Island within the reef-fringed western lagoon, Mutton Bird Island to the east, Gower to the south, and, ten miles or so to the southeast, Balls Pyramid, a precipitous sliver of rock which rises almost two thousand feet from a base less than an acre in size. Geologists believe that Lord Howe and most of its outriders were once part of a long volcanic chain that stretched from New Zealand to New Caledonia.

Lieutenant Henry Lidgbird Ball, in command of *Supply* en route to Norfolk with Philip Gidley King's party in 1788, was the first to sight Lord Howe, and he named it after the First Sea Lord of the time. There was no indication of previous occupation by any race of man. The only mammals were bats, there were few reptiles, and the remarkable feature of the island was an amazing profusion of vegetation and birdlife, much of it endemic to the island and occurring nowhere else in the world – indicating prolonged isolation and freedom from predators. Many species, especially among the birds, have become entirely extinct since the island was discovered, due mainly to depredations by early whalers and the alien mammals – rats, cats, pigs and goats – which they introduced to the island.

Looking south to Mounts Lidgbird and Gower, Lord Howe Island. These twin peaks are remnants of ancient volcanoes. Lord Howe is a crescent-shaped island, six miles long and rarely more than a mile wide. Ned's Beach is in the foreground of this picture, and the shallow main lagoon lies in the curve of the crescent and the shelter of the mountains.

Moonlight, romance and Howea palms on Ned's Beach, Lord Howe Island.

The Admiralty Islets lie to the north of Lord
Howe. They are nesting places for gannets,
sooty terns and bosun birds.

Shells of Lord Howe Island.

Banyan trees, Ficus columnaris, send down
trailing curtains of aerial roots, turning the
sheltered central forests into an area
of perpetual twilight.

A remarkable example of wind currents
and cloud development over Mount
Gower; cold winds from Antartica hit
the warm mountains, forming clouds
while you watch.

Islands near Port Stephens. Right: "Tied"
islands, mountains isolated by rising seas
and later reunited to the mainland by
drifting sand. Above: Broughton Island
(top picture) and Cabbage Tree Island
(centre), are wildlife reserves.

The first settlers on Lord Howe were three whalers, their Maori wives and two children. They built homes near what is now called Old Settlement and grew vegetables, which they traded to crews of visiting whalers. A few years later Owen Poole and Richard Dawson bought these people out and began a regular provisioning service for passing ships. A small settlement was formed though the population did not number over a hundred until early this century. During these first fifty years the mainland government took little notice of the islanders, and a vague communal system developed. Unwritten laws governed behaviour, property boundaries and prices for produce. When the end of whaling as a profitable industry spelt the end of Lord Howe as a provisioning port, an export trade was developed of the seed of the Kentia (Howea) palm; the islanders gathered them communally and shared the revenue communally. (In recent years this industry has been largely replaced by tourism, but every islander still receives by birthright a share of the island's income from palm-seeds.) Lack of documentation of land holdings was a cause of much grievance, and in 1953 the Lord Howe Island Act was passed. A clause in this Act prevents newcomers from purchasing land; they must "marry" in to become legal inhabitants, with the right to work on the island, though a person of independent means can become a "permanent" resident of a guest house. Islanders pay no rent or land taxes, though adult males have another birthright – the obligation to spend a certain number of days each year on public works (or pay another to do this for them).

Nobbys, near Newcastle, and Lion Island, in Broken Bay, are peaks of former hills isolated by rising seas; one has been "tied" once again to the coast, the other remains an island.

The flora of the offshore islands is similar to that of the mainland. Top picture: Angophoras and grass-trees, Lion Island. Lower pictures, left to right: Darwinia fascicularis, Lambertia formosa, and the "red gums", Angophora costata, are common on the rocky hillsides; native pigface, Carpobrotus aequilaterus, grows on the sandy shores.

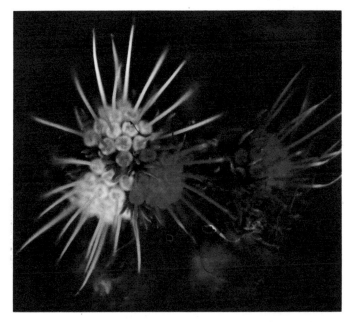

Bushfire haze over The Tollgates, an almost continuous line of small rocky islands which barricade the entrance to Bateman's Bay.

ISLANDS OF THE TASMAN SEA

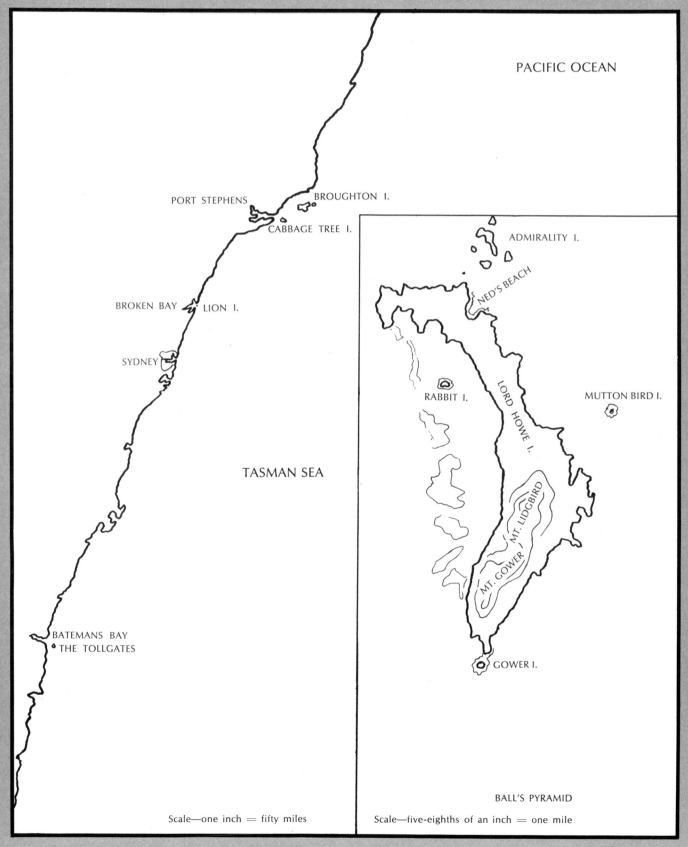

PACIFIC OCEAN

PORT STEPHENS

BROUGHTON I.

CABBAGE TREE I.

ADMIRALITY I.

NED'S BEACH

BROKEN BAY   LION I.

SYDNEY

RABBIT I.

LORD HOWE I.

MUTTON BIRD I.

TASMAN SEA

MT. LIDGBIRD

MT. GOWER

BATEMANS BAY
THE TOLLGATES

GOWER I.

BALL'S PYRAMID

Scale—one inch = fifty miles   Scale—five-eighths of an inch = one mile

Norfolk Island · Christmas Island · Heard Island · McDonald Island
Cocos Keeling Island · New Guinea

AUSTRALIA'S ISLAND TERRITORIES

Goroka warrior from the central highlands of New Guinea, in full regalia.

Heard and McDonald, Australian island territories on the fringe of Antartica.

Australia's island territories range from tropical Papua-New Guinea, which lies within the equatorial zone and covers an area of 180,000 square miles, to Heard and McDonald Islands, frozen volcanoes on the fringe of Antarctica. They include Cocos (Keeling) Islands, two atolls – rings of small coral cays – in the Indian Ocean, about halfway between Perth and Ceylon. Here Scottish sailor John Clunies Ross established a settlement in 1825, and became the first of the "Kings of the Cocos." Here Charles Darwin formulated his theories on coral reefs, based on observations made during his visit to the islands on *Beagle* in 1836. It was from these islands that George Clunies Ross, the third "king," in 1888 made the first settlement on Christmas Island, some five hundred miles to the east and now also an island territory of Australia. It was from these islands that the dramatic World War I signal "SOS *Emden* here" led to the destruction of that dreaded German raider. She was intercepted by HMAS *Sydney,* whose captain sent the equally famous signal *"Emden* beached and done for" when the raider, engulfed in flames, ran aground on North Keeling Island.

Christmas Island appears to owe its name to a Captain Mynors of the Dutch East India Company, who sighted it on Christmas Day, 1643, but it was marked on Dutch maps much earlier, and the first European to sight it seems to have been British mariner Richard Rowe who reported its existence in 1615; Dampier is said to have been the first European to land there, in 1688. It was surveyed by HMS *Flying Fish* in 1887, settled from Cocos in 1888, and formally annexed by Britain the same year. The surveys had revealed the island to be remarkably rich in vegetation, birdlife – and phosphates. As a result of exploitation of the latter, the former have suffered widespread destruction. Phosphate, formed from the interaction of seabird droppings and coral, is unfortunately an extractive industry – its exploitation can lead not only to the disappearance of distinctive flora and fauna but also to the island itself, given time. Around the turn of this century, Professor Wood Jones deplored the destruction: "Before the inrush of all the turmoil of wealth-getting, the wonderful fauna had to give way," he wrote. "Christmas Island has become a remarkably successful undertaking, but as a preserve for an interesting and isolated fauna, and as an ideal place for a peaceful and happy community, its day has passed."

Norfolk Island, almost one thousand miles northeast of Sydney, was Australia's first island territory and the site of the second British settlement in the Pacific. It is a hilly, fertile island, volcanic in origin, dominated by straight towering pines and sheer rugged cliffs. In size it is roughly five miles by three, and, apart from its two tiny uninhabited satellite islands, it is isolated by four or five hundred miles or more from its nearest neighbours in the South Pacific – New Caledonia, New Zealand, and Lord Howe Island. Captain James Cook, in command of *Resolution* on his second voyage round

the world, brought back the first account. He saw
in the tall pines, masts and spars for the British Fleet,
and in the native flax which grew in profusion,
canvas for the ships' sails. He "found the Island
uninhabited and near a kin to New Zealand . . .
the chief product . . . Spruce Pines which grow
here in vast abundance and to a vast size, from two
to three feet diameter and upwards, it is of a
different sort to those in New Caledonia and also
to those in New Zealand and for Masts, Yards &ca
superior to both. We cut down one of the smallest
trees we could find and Cut a length from the
uper end to make a Topgt Mast or Yard . . . Here
then is a nother Isle where Masts for the largest
Ships may be had. Here are the same sort of
Pigions, Parrots and Parrokeets as in New Zealand,
Rails and some small birds. The Sea fowl are
White Boobies, guls, Terns &ca which breed
undisturbed on the Rocks and in the Clifts. The
coast is not distitute of Fish, our people caught
some which were excellent . . . I took posission of
this Isle as I had done of all the others we had
discovered, and named it *Norfolk Isle,* in honour
of that noble family . . ."

Cook's glowing reports caused the British
Government to instruct Arthur Phillip, in command
of the First Fleet and the penal colony at Botany
Bay, "as soon as circumstances will admit of it,
to send a small establishment thither." So the
Governor accordingly despatched Lieutenant
Philip Gidley King in HMS *Supply,* within a week of
the official establishment of the settlement at
Sydney Cove. They arrived at Norfolk on March 1st,
and, after circling the island for five days searching
for a safe landing place, finally found a passage
through the reef and went ashore at Kingston,
the only place on the coastline where cliffs give
way to a sandy beach. Here the second British
settlement in the Pacific was set up. The felling of
the pines provided pastures for wheat and timber
for buildings. The sloop in which Bass and Flinders
sailed round Tasmania, was built of Norfolk pine.

North coast of Heard Island and the bowsprit of Patanela, *ship of the 1964-65 South Indian Ocean Expedition there. The ship's name is a West Tasmanian Aboriginal word, "spirit of the storm".*

Sea-elephants, Macrorhinus proboscideus, *and king penguins,* Aptenodytes patagonica, *are re-establishing themselves on these islands after being almost wiped out by sealers in the closing decades of last century. Southern skua gull,* Catharacta lonnbergi, *guards its chick.*

Rugged coastline, Christmas Island; brown booby gannet, Sula leucogaster.

Old gaol and administrative block at Kingston, framed by Norfolk Island pines. Phillip Island is in the background.

Below: The row of graceful arches, known as The Stables. These are relics of the convict days when Norfolk was a place of "extremest punishment short of Death." Some of these convict-built structures are intact, others have been restored, but many are mere shells. Pitcairners, who came at a later period of the island's history, "quarried" the abandoned buildings for foundations and chimney-stones, and paving for pig-pens.

Cattle graze amidst the ruins; they have right-of-way everywhere, even in the main street. Below: Mighty pines of Norfolk.

The ill-fated La Pérouse, who anchored off Norfolk on his way to Botany Bay and his last contact with fellow-Europeans, described the island (on which he was unable to land because of heavy surf) as "only a place fit for angels and eagles to reside in." The British authorities obviously did not agree, for they soon transformed it into a place fit for neither. The brown-headed petrels which once nested annually on the island in astronomical numbers could probably fit into both categories. They earned the name "birds of Providence" in 1790, when their arrival, "thick as a shower of hail" on their traditional breeding grounds, coincided with famine and starvation following the wreck of the Sirius and the failure of two other supply ships to reach the island from Sydney. Almost two hundred thousand of these birds were slaughtered in the following three months. These settlers undoubtedly owed their lives to the Providence petrels, but though they acknowledged the debt in the name they gave them, there was to be no thanksgiving amnesty in other less drastic times. The birds, blindly returning annually to their home "fit only for eagles or angels" were utterly exterminated within a decade. The second penal settlement was a place, not for angels, but "of extremest punishment short of Death," marked by treadmill, rack and triangle, murder and mutiny – a brutal and terrible place from which the sternest angel would surely flee in horror. Norfolk today is a peaceful island. The old convict ruins dream in the sun amid meadows marked by flowering hedges and winding stone walls. In valleys too steep for cultivation king ferns grow, and tall hibiscus-flowered white oaks keep company with the lofty pines. Phillip Island, ravaged by rabbits into a barren mass of purple, red and orange gravel, has nonetheless a glory all its own, and glows in the sun's rays like a fiery opal. Though tourism is the main trade, this is an island on the way to nowhere, where ships and planes call "weather permitting"; life still follows the leisurely pace of the islanders, born of the Bounty mutiny and brought from Pitcairn when the penal settlement was abandoned in the eighteen-fifties. These descendants of English sailors and their Tahitian wives pay no rates and taxes. They have a patois of their own – a mixture of old West Country English and Tahitian – though all speak excellent English also. They live in a seeming paradise, so perhaps La Pérouse was right, after all.

The old cemetery by the sea's edge marches into the sandhills. Tombstones record the fate of convicts — "executed . . . executed" — and of their gaolers who lie beside them: "Barbarously murdered . . . killed by a fall . . ."

The Bloody Bridge. Beyond the Kingston cemetery, where the land rises and the sandhills give place to cliffs, this stone bridge spans a small stream. Legend says that the convicts building it, driven to despair by a brutal warder, slew him and walled up his body in the structure, on their return telling a tale that he had gone to the cliff's edge and not come back. Blood seeping through the stonework exposed the deed and gave the bridge its melancholy title.

NORFOLK ISLAND

BIRD ROCK

CASCADE BAY

AIRFIELD

KINGSTON

BLOODY BRIDGE

BALL BAY

SYDNEY BAY

Scale—one inch = one and one third miles ⚓ NEPEAN I.

HEARD ISLAND

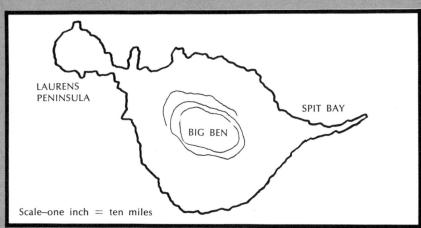

LAURENS PENINSULA

BIG BEN

SPIT BAY

Scale—one inch = ten miles

CHRISTMAS ISLAND

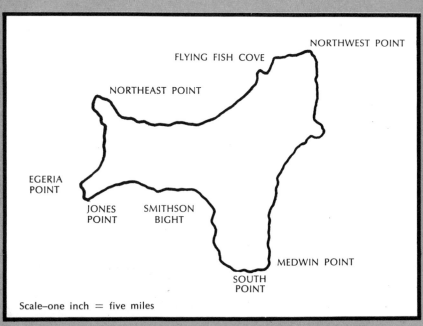

NORTHWEST POINT

FLYING FISH COVE

NORTHEAST POINT

EGERIA POINT

JONES POINT

SMITHSON BIGHT

MEDWIN POINT

SOUTH POINT

Scale—one inch = five miles

PAPUA & NEW GUINEA

New Guinea sing-sing, a festival of colour and frenzy. Both men and women take part; bodies are richly decorated with pearlshell, feathers and ochre, and they dance to the beat of hollow wooden "hour-glass" drums slapped with the hand.

Ceremonial mask of the Sepik River people. The sculpture of this district, dynamic and often grotesque, features human and bird figures of exaggerated form.

Highland boys fold their arms and hug themselves to keep warm at Goroka. Nights are chilly even in the tropics, when the altitude is over five thousand feet.

New Guinea, second largest island in the world (only Greenland has a greater area), stretches from the equator to the immediate north of Australia. The Territory of Papua-New Guinea forms the eastern half, and includes also numerous adjacent islands – New Britain, New Ireland, Bougainville and Manus are the largest, and the many smaller ones include the Schouten Islands, the Trobriands, the Louisiades Archipelago and the D'Entrecasteaux Group. The dominating feature of the main island is the mountainous spine which lies along the centre, rising in places to a height of over 15,000 feet and dividing the island into north and south. These mountains are not a continuous single chain, but rather a complex system of ranges, often separated by broad and grassy valleys and, in some cases, extending to the coast and even across the sea to the adjacent islands.

From the highlands flow many mighty rivers: the Sepik, in the north, and the Fly, in the south, are navigable for hundreds of miles by ships of medium size. Other great rivers are the Ramu and the Markham in the north, and the Turama, Kikori and Purari in the south. In the generally high rainfall of the area, these fast-flowing rivers carry great volumes of water in all seasons, and form barriers which divide the terrain as much as the broken ranges do. All carry vast amounts of silt which has, over centuries, reclaimed from the sea fan-shaped deltas of mudbanks and low-lying islands, so that the major rivers are lost in a mosaic of swamps, channels and mangrove-held flats. In most mountain districts rain is practically incessant. Clouds perpetually shroud the higher peaks and the greater part of the island is covered with thick rainforest – a dense canopy of tall trees topping a tangled understory of creepers and vines. These swamps and jungles, rivers, gorges and mountain barriers effectively isolate regions, so that biologically speaking New Guinea could be said to consist of islands within an island – districts so cut off from neighbouring areas that their isolation is no less than that of islands separated by seas. Nowhere are these differences so marked as in the social organisation, attitudes and even physical characteristics of the inhabitants, and the casual visitor, meeting and speaking with the gentle people of one area, may well be bewildered by tales of treachery and aggressiveness told of the inhabitants from another region.

Young virgins of Nondugl, in the Western Highlands, carry hams to market. (The wide waistbands indicate virginity.)

Tree-climbing kangaroo, Dendrolagus ursinus; ungainly on land, they clamber through dense jungle with amazing speed.

Native lads sort harvested passionfruit at Goroka. Though introduced, these fruit now grow wild over the casuarinas.

Below: Moonlight over Madang Harbour.

Poinciana trees frame Port Moresby, administrative centre of the Territory.

Wahgi Valley, Central Highlands, seen from Goroka. Moss festoons the forests of cloud-shrouded Mount Michael, seen in the background.

Nondugl, in the Western Highlands, site of an experimental sheep station in the nineteen-fifties. Annual rainfall is heavy, and Romney Marsh sheep were used, which are adaptable to very wet conditions. However the project was not successful.

Native children at Port Moresby. Education was until recently limited to primary schooling; secondary education was begun in the nineteen-fifties, and the University of Papua and New Guinea was established several years later in 1965.

The people of Wogeo (a true island, one of the largest of the Schouten Group) believe that the earth is like a shallow saucer, with Wogeo at its centre. They maintain that Wogeo alone has existed always; in the beginning it was surrounded by empty ocean, but later, as windblown canoes brought evidence of other lands, the myths were amended to cover creation of new islands by their culture heroes. This philosophy underlines the insularity of the divergent tribes of the land and sea islands of Papua-New Guinea.

The stereotyped image of headhunting cannibals reflects the tribes which had the greatest impact on headhunting Europeans, seeking indentured labour for plantations. In contrast, consider the gentle Arapesh, who live in a society where warfare is practically unknown, and those who have killed are not glorified but rather looked upon with discomfort. The whole outlook is orientated to "growing" things – yams, pigs and especially children. A father's claim to his child is not that he begot it, but that he has fed it, and this concept is carried through into the marriage customs. Girls and boys are betrothed as children and the girl then goes to live in the home of her future husband. Here the boy's family continue to "grow" the bride who, from this time on, moves freely between her home of origin and her husband's home, leading essentially the same life in both, and forming the same warm attachment to the boy's family as to her own. The long years that the boy and girl live together as brother and sister determine the general attitude towards sex as essentially domestic; even in this field, competition and struggle are alien to the Arapesh. All trade is disguised as gift exchange; there is no encouragement given to the building up of a surplus of goods, and any such surplus is socialised for the benefit of the whole community. The Arapesh see no reason for anyone to be other than mild and gentle; they will placate a violent man and give him what he wants rather than sacrifice the general peace. But despite this seeming permissiveness, the aggressive or aquisitive personality has a sorry time among the Arapesh. By the insistence that all people are good and gentle, that neither men nor women are strongly sexed, that no-one has any other motive except to grow yams and children, the Arapesh refuse to take such temperaments seriously. The society actually gives quite a lot of leeway to violence, but gives no meaning to it. With no place for strong leadership, for individual exploits of bravery and strength in warfare, or initiative and competitiveness in commerce, such men find themselves treated as almost insane.

Big sing-sing at Nondugl. Flamboyant bird-of-paradise plumes decorate the headdresses of the warriors. People walk great distances from the surrounding hills to attend these ceremonial occasions, and may spend months in the preparation of the elaborate and colourful decorations.

NEW GUINEA

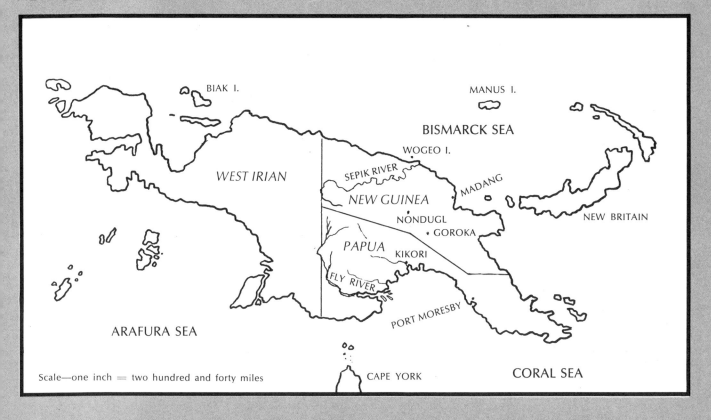

Scale—one inch = two hundred and forty miles

Index

Scientific names and names of ships are in italics; page references in bold type refer to illustrations.

Acknowledgements

The authors wish to extend their sincere thanks to the following —Nandjawarra, O.B.E., of Groote Eylandt, and many other Aboriginal friends; Colonel Michael Casey of Groote Eylandt, Rev. Shepherdson of Elcho Island, Rev. Doug Belcher of Mornington Island, Rev. Sherlock; Mr Giese and Mr Milliken of the Welfare Department, Darwin; Professor John Cawte, Miss Elizabeth Pope, the Director and staff of the Australian Museum, Dr Mary Tindale, the Director and staff of the National Herbarium of New South Wales, Dr. D. L. Serventy, Vincent Serventy, Eric Worrell; the late Sir Edward Hallstrom, Peter Baillieu, Dick Dumbrell, Ron Milne, Geoff Goddard, Sandra and Oke Blomquist, John Barrie; Tom Watson, Jeremy Long, Fred Sutton, Vic Parkinson; Elaine Baglin and Bill Mullins; Maureen McGrath and Enid Dumbrell; Eddie Connellan of Connellan Airways, Jack Hunt and Don Adams of Island Airways, Helmit Apitz, Dr John Morris, Jack Parker and the many other intrepid seamen and pilots who made the book possible. Photographs of Heard Island were taken by members of the South Indian Ocean Expedition to Heard Island, 1964-65.